SHORT CUTS

INTRODUCTIONS TO FILM STUDIES

OTHER SELECT TITLES IN THE SHORT CUTS SERIES

FILM CENSORSHIP

REGULATING AMERICA'S SCREEN

SHERI CHINEN BIESEN

WALLFLOWER

LONDON and NEW YORK

A Wallflower Press book
Published by
Columbia University Press
Publishers Since 1893
New York • Chichester, West Sussex
cup.columbia.edu

Wallflower Press® is a registered trademark of Columbia University Press

Cataloging-in-Publication Data is available from the Library of Congress

ISBN 978-0-231-18313-0 (pbk. : alk. paper)
ISBN 978-0-231-85113-8 (e-book)

Columbia University Press books are printed on permanent and durable acid-free paper.
Printed in the United States of America

Cover image: *The Outlaw* (1943) © RKO Radio Pictures Inc.

CONTENTS

ACKNOWLEDGEMENTS

This journey exploring the world of Hollywood film censorship began nearly twenty years ago and is greatly indebted to many people. I would like to especially thank Yoram Allon, editorial director at Wallflower Press, and all the staff there and at Columbia University Press for their kind efforts that enabled this project to come to fruition. Special thanks to Ned Comstock and the archival staff at the USC Cinematic Arts Library Special Collections, Academy of Motion Picture Arts and Sciences Margaret Herrick Library Center for Motion Picture Study, MPPDA Digital Archive at Flinders University, Digital Media History Library, USC Warner Bros. Archive, UCLA Young Research Arts Library Special Collections, Harry Ransom Humanities Research Center at the University of Texas, New York Public Library for the Performing Arts Special Collections, Library of Congress, American Film Institute, British Film Institute, Indiana University Lilly Library, National Archives, and Museum of Modern Art for their research assistance. I would also like to thank Brian Neve, Brian Taves, Thomas Doherty, Richard B. Jewell, Drew Casper, Leonard Leff, Clayton Koppes, Richard Maltby, Garth Jowett, Charles Maland, Scott Curtis, Eric Hoyt, Matthew Bernstein, Thomas Schatz, Nicholas Cull, Fred Metchick, Peter Rollins, Jim Welsh, Walter Metz, Steven Carr, Cynthia Baron, Rebecca Martin, Julie Grossman, Paula Musegades, Mark Williams, Mary Desjardins, Shelley Stamp, Mahinder Kingra, Peter Lev, Peter Kunze, Joseph Bierman, Richard Grupenhoff, Keith Brand, my colleagues and students at Rowan University, Nate Chinen, John Gizis, my family and grandparents.

INTRODUCTION

Hollywood censorship of motion pictures was on the minds of many Americans on December 19, 2014. Two days earlier, a major studio had withdrawn the release of a provocative film because of outrage, cyber hacking, and threats of theater attacks from a foreign government. At a national press conference, US President Barack Obama insisted, 'We cannot have a society in which some dictator someplace can start imposing censorship here in the United States.'[1] When Sony Pictures cancelled the release of controversial black comedy *The Interview* after theatre chains refused to screen it, media industry watchers expressed concern about the potential censorship implications of restricting First Amendment 'free speech' in curtailing the release of a film. 'Sony Drops *The Interview* Following Terrorist Threats,' Brooks Barnes and Michael Cieply of the *New York Times* reported.[2] 'Over the 48 hours after it pulled the film,' Peter Elkind of *Fortune* magazine observed, 'Sony again became a target, as critics from Hollywood to Washington voiced alarm that the studio had caved.' President Obama asserted that Sony studio 'made a mistake.' Author Stephen King wrote, 'Sony's decision to pull *The Interview* is unsettling in so many ways.' He added: 'Good thing they didn't publish *The Satanic Verses*.'[3] (Sony later released the film digitally on Netflix and other internet video on demand [VOD] streaming sites and at a few theaters.)

However, despite the controversy and ratings battles over the content of specific films, many do not even realise that the motion picture production and reception climate for contemporary American cinema is quite different than in the earlier classic era of the Hollywood studio system 'Golden Age' in which film censorship thrived. Moreover, today's American films are not actually censored in the way they were during the height of the classical Hollywood studio system of the 1930s, 1940s and 1950s under a codified system of film censorship which unraveled by the 1960s after the demise of the Motion Picture Production Code.

Although the term 'censorship' is invoked in contemporary parlance, there is in fact a distinction between official federal censorship enforced by the government, versus a voluntary system of self-censorship regulation enforced by the motion picture industry as in classical Hollywood, versus unofficial efforts by a studio to constrain film content to secure a desired rating or market a film in a global arena. In this context, the ideal legal climate for censorship in the United States has dissipated since the Supreme Court's rulings (Mutual vs. Ohio case and its overturning with The Miracle decision) laid the groundwork for First Amendment 'free speech' battles which would eventually allow for greater latitude with regard to film content. This study, then, aims to elucidate these distinctions and clarify these issues and provide insight into specific historical instances that are not typically considered in which Hollywood screen censorship constrained the content, production, distribution, exhibition and reception of American films.

This concise, introductory book on Hollywood censorship history explores US film regulation from the early silent cinema period through the classical studio system era to the Production Code's demise in the 1960s and the ratings system in post-classical Hollywood. Methodologically, this book relies on extensive primary archival research to historically contextualise these censorship issues throughout American film history. The scope and substance of the book historically spans the early silent film period, pre-Code era, film industry self-censorship, government regulation and propaganda during World War II, the post-war breakdown of censorship through the late-1960s into the New Hollywood era to focus on efforts to regulate Hollywood film content. Topics include: the Mutual vs. Ohio Case (1915), Jazz Age Prohibition years, controversial or banned productions, establishment of the Motion Picture Producers and Distributors of

America Association (MPPDA), lobbying by major religious groups against Hollywood, Motion Picture Production Code, the 'Hays Office' Production Code Administration (PCA) and industry self-censorship, lapses in enforcement, World War II federal government propaganda efforts of the Office of War Information (OWI) Bureau of Motion Pictures, major challenges to the Production Code, The Miracle Case and easing of regulation in the 1950s-1960s, establishment of a ratings system in 1968 and the legacy of the PCA in later years vis-à-vis efforts to control film content after the Code's demise.

The methods and concerns of film industry censorship in the United States provide insight in understanding censorship in other international countries today, whether Iran or China, Russia or nations in Europe. For example, Iranian director Abbas Kiarostami commented on screen censorship in Iran: 'It's no use thinking you can change the world with a film and it's mad to make a film knowing in advance that it'll be censored and will never be allowed to be shown. An artist should go as far as society will let him. Having made a film that's banned is the same as never having made it, so much so that you need to know what power the government has.' Kiarostami further observed: 'I think you have to come to terms with censorship, accept it. We filmmakers, we're intellectuals and we ought to know what kind of government's governing us and the kind of audience we're working for.' In considering the political censorship problems faced during the period of the Islamic Revolution, he insisted, 'We're in the Middle East, in the Third World ... We need time; we want to advance in stages ... That's why I believe in the simple films I make, for I think that, little by little, they're working towards a better future.'[4]

Because of the importance of the international market, especially Europe and Latin America, Hollywood studios were concerned during World War II, for example, with censorship in other countries, ranging from democracies like the United Kingdom to totalitarian regimes like Hitler's Germany. Furthermore, European filmmakers fleeing Nazi Germany and other countries played an important role in American cinema as talented émigré artists, writers, actors, directors and other creative personnel such as Billy Wilder, Fritz Lang, Robert Siodmak, Alfred Hitchcock, Fred Zinnemann, and Peter Lorre made extraordinary contributions to the art of motion pictures in the classic Hollywood studio era. America's motion picture industry was also influenced by Soviet cinema and European filmmaking, which had its own complex censorship history, yet produced remarkable cinematic imagery as seen in the powerful montage editing techniques of Sergei Eisenstein (who came to Hollywood and worked at Paramount in 1930) and Dziga Vertov (whose brother was Hollywood cinematographer Boris Kaufman, who won an Oscar for Elia Kazan's *On the Waterfront*) and popularity of classical Hollywood montage sequences and other avant-garde techniques incorporated into US cinema by talented European émigré filmmakers like Slavko Vorkapich and Oskar Fischinger.

International directors recounted stories of censorship. Alfred Hitchcock recalled British censors banning screen depictions of insanity. Hitchcock pushed the envelope of screen censorship with films of perverse psychology, comparing them to a 'nightmare'. Hitchcock admitted: 'I have tried...to show sex in its amusing and exotic and erotic aspects [although] I've never had much nudity in my films... I merely suggest that they are nude, because you have to leave something to the audience's imagination. The same thing is true, I think, for violence.' He explained, 'The whole design of *Psycho* was to reduce the violence on the screen as the film progressed and to increase the sense of violence in the audience's mind... the cocking of the knife, the girl's face and the feet and everything was so rapid that there were 78 separate pieces of film in 45 seconds.' Hitchcock insisted, 'Everyone's waiting for the one great scene on a super-sized Cinerama screen of the ultimate sexual scene...Well, I've done that... In *North by Northwest*, at the end, I have Cary Grant and Eva Marie Saint in the same train berth and then in the very next scene, which is also the last scene of the film, I have the long train entering a dark tunnel.'[5]

Akira Kurosawa described how he hated censors in Japan during the war years. He had to gain endorsement from the Imperial Army, Navy and Ministry of the Interior and faced censorship during the conflict and the subsequent Allied occupation.[6] Kurosawa criticised Japanese wartime censors, calling them 'obsessive maniacs who treated us like criminals', yet characterised post-war American censors as 'humane and genuinely seeking communication', although his 1945 film *Men Who Tread On the Tiger's Tail* was banned by Japanese censors as a 'travesty of the classic [Kabuki] theatre' and US censors continued the ban until 1952, two years after Kurosawa's international critical acclaim for his 1950 film *Rashomon*.[7] In retrospect, Kurosawa admitted, 'The censors were so far gone as to find the following sentence obscene: "The factory gate waited for the student workers, thrown open in longing." What can I say? This obscenity verdict was handed down by a censor in response to my script for my 1944 film about a girls' volunteer corps, *Ichiban utsukushiku* (*The Most Beautiful*) ... I could not fathom what was ... obscene about this sentence ... But for the mentally disturbed censor this sentence was unquestionably obscene.' He called this kind of censorship, 'nothing more or less than a case of sexual pathology'.[8] (Note the contrasting views of Kurosawa versus Hitchcock on the use of cinematic sexual innuendo to subvert screen censorship.) Moreover, in 1954 collaborator Tomoyuki Tanaka—who produced Kurosawa's *Yojimbo*, *Sanjuro*, *High and Low*, *Red Beard*, and *Kagemusha*—and Toho studio wanted to make a Japanese-Indonesian co-production *Eiko-no Kagi-ni* (*In the Shadow of Glory*) about the aftermath of the Japanese occupation of Indonesia, but anti-Japanese sentiment and political pressure in Indonesia forced the government to deny visas for the Japanese filmmakers, which nixed the film project.[9]

In America, during the earlier classical studio system era, Hollywood films often faced a gender-racial-sexuality-bias in US film industry censorial organisations and in their representational constraints. In particular, the majority of Hollywood film censors were men, regulating screen images to determine how women, sexuality and people of colour were cinematically portrayed. Moreover, Hollywood's censorial regulation of 'difference' further marginalised already oppressed minorities.[10] For example, Hollywood's industry censorship 'moral blueprint,' the Motion Picture Production Code, banned the screen depiction of interracial and homosexual relationships outright, prohibited adulterous romantic sexual affairs, and marginalised people of colour onscreen, often objectifying and constraining women's roles to encourage feminine domesticity, sexual appeal to men, and heterosexual marriage. As a result of these censorial constraints, cinematic signification would also convey 'coded' hidden meaning to suggest what could not be shown onscreen. To the degree that it was possible at the time, filmmakers like Billy Wilder, Otto Preminger, George Cukor, Fred Zinnemann, and Elia Kazan, challenged political and 'moral' Hollywood studio system industry censorship regulating 'difference' as they explored issues of cultural/ethnic/sexual identity and the problems minorities confronted in an oppressive society. Facing political oppression and censorship, many European émigrés fleeing fascism overseas were dedicated to social realism and these persecuted talents coming to the United States often supported the American Popular Front against fascism. As cultural historian Michael Sherry explains, émigrés like Billy Wilder and Elia Kazan, as well as African-American jazz musician Duke Ellington, Jewish American composer Leonard Bernstein, gay director George Cukor, and others formed a 'new generation of plebeian artists and intellectuals...rooted in the Popular Front politics of the 1930s and linked to the rise of mass culture.'[11]

Recalling the classical Hollywood studio system's industry self-censorship of films, director George Cukor opined, 'I think censorship is tough. The great dilemma is that it is also a question of taste. I believe censorship was brought on by bad taste', where a film could have nothing sexy or immoral in it, but is so vulgar that it is nonetheless censored. Known for his wonderful direction of screen actor performances, especially women stars, such as Katharine Hepburn in *The Philadelphia Story* (1940) and Judy Garland with James Mason in *A Star is Born* (1954), Cukor insisted: 'I'll tell you what they *cannot* censor: thought. Now, I've found that very interesting—that you can *think* anything—and they can't cut that out. And that's what I think of all the great ones.' Praising Mae West's cinematic 'delicacy' and 'inference', he added: 'I mean Elvis Presley—whom I consider great—and Marilyn Monroe; their brains were uncensored. They could imagine all kinds of things and there was really nothing immoral about it. Quite different—and I thought much more subtle than it is now.'[12]

To contextualise these observations from directors who faced screen censorship, although primary archival research sources are typically stronger evidentiary support for scholarly arguments than oral histories (which can often be less accurate or factually reliable than other primary sources), such insightful points of view are revealing. These filmmaking perspectives demonstrate the different kinds of screen censorship and an array of attitudes and approaches to film censorship. Moreover, Hollywood film censorship influenced screen censorship overseas, including British film censorship. It is thus important to understand the various efforts to censor and constrain American film content from the classical studio system to New Hollywood cinema, and it is with this aim in mind that I have written this concise volume, situating the rich history of censorship through extensive primary archival research.[13]

1   PRE-CODE ERA

In the United States during the early decades of the twentieth century, in the comparatively lax 'pre-Code' era, religious and civic organisations expressed concern over motion pictures regarding their corrupting potential to influence impressionable youth. In this emergent regulatory climate, debates ensued over whether there should be self-regulation of screen content by the movie industry or by an outside censorship organisation such as the government.

Concerns, public outcry, controversy and censorship efforts regarding the content of American films arose in the earliest days of silent motion pictures. As early as the 1890s, sexual suggestiveness in 'peep show' movies was considered scandalous in such films as James White's infamous short subject, *The Kiss* (1896). Partial nudity was revealed and tolerated in masculine boxing movies and body building shorts, such as *Sandow: the Strong Man* (1894), showing off ample displays of male flesh. However, even fully-dressed women were considered sexual and provocative if they danced alluringly in 'exotic' ethnic attire, as in the suggestive gyrations of *Fatima's Coochee-Coochee Dance* (1896), in which censor bars actually appear in the film to cover the scantily-clad breasts, shoulders and shaking hips of the belly dancer that *Phonoscope* magazine called 'the poetry of motion'.[14]

By 1897, the US State of Maine endeavoured to ban boxing movies to prohibit the screening of the heavyweight championship documentary, *The*

Fatima's Coochee-Coochee Dance [uncensored]. (New York Public Library/ MOMA, 1896)

Fatima's Coochee-Coochee Dance [censored bars]. New York Public Library/MOMA, 1896)

Corbett-Fitzsimmons Fight (1897), since prizefighting was illegal in most states, with the exception of Nevada.[15] Efforts at industry self-regulation began in these early years of cinema. Thomas Edison denounced and attempted to restrict boxing films in the 1890s and the Motion Picture Patents Company (MPPC, known as 'the Trust') and the National Board of Censorship of Motion Pictures (NBC, later renamed National Board of Review of Motion Pictures [NBR] in 1915) attempted to avoid official government censorship by federal, state and local entities in 1909 by initiating internal industry self-regulation of films.[16] Nevertheless, different kinds of censorship emerged during this early cinema era. Boxing pictures were censored (after black fighter Jack Johnson defeated white champ Jim Jeffries, prompting riots) when Congress passed the Sims Act federal censorship law in 1912, which banned fight films as interstate commerce, the first time the US government enforced censorship affecting US distribution of motion pictures.[17] Moreover, the Motion Picture Patents Company also enacted trade restrictions against Pathé (in France) and other foreign film companies, which reveals how American censorship, even in its very origins, had a global awareness and impetus.[18]

Early silent-era films pushed the boundaries of Hollywood screen content. D.W. Griffith's crime short, *The Musketeers of Pig Alley* (1912), featured an irreverent gangster cynically defying and outwitting the law. The National Association for the Advancement of Colored People (NAACP) protested racist images in Griffith's controversial Civil War epic, *Birth of a Nation* (1915), which incited riots in Pennsylvania, Ohio, Massachusetts and Colorado. In Cecil B. DeMille's provocative illicit romance, *The Cheat* (1915), a wealthy Japanese lord (Sessue Hayakawa) becomes embroiled in an adulterous, interracial sex affair as he tries to seduce and rape a married woman (Fanny Ward), engages in a violent tussle, then provocatively grabs her hair, rips her dress and brands her flesh with a searing iron. By February

Sessue Hayakawa brands Fanny Ward in *The Cheat*. (Famous Players-Lasky, 1915)

9

1916, the Japanese Association of Southern California formally protested the Los Angeles City Council against showing *The Cheat*. In November 1918, Paramount re-issued *The Cheat* with Hayakawa's Japanese character Hishuru Tori changed to Burmese descent and renamed Haka Arakau, to avoid bad political relations between the United States and World War I ally Japan.

Mutual vs. Ohio and Censor Boards

Film regulation developed in the formative years of silent cinema. Local municipal censorship boards were established, such as the Chicago Board of Censors in 1907; other cities and states followed. New York City, a major film market, passed municipal film censorship laws in 1906 and 1913. States such as Pennsylvania (in 1911), then Kansas and Ohio (in 1913) and Maryland (in 1916) established state film censorship laws and film review boards which issued permits for moral and proper productions and withheld permits for inappropriate films. By 1915, the *Mutual vs. Ohio* US Supreme Court Decision, supporting Ohio's state censorship board, created an ideal legal climate for screen censorship in the United States by denying motion pictures the First Amendment free speech protection given the press.[19]

Mutual Film Corporation, a Detroit company that leased films to Midwestern states, sought to overturn Ohio's state censorship policies, claiming the system violated free speech, First Amendment and other freedom guarantees in Ohio's constitution. However, the United States Supreme Court rejected this claim and declared that films are capable of 'evil' in attractiveness and manner of exhibition and ruled that motion pictures are a business, pure and simple, conducted for profit, not an art form, not a medium deserving free speech and therefore not eligible for constitutional protection. (This ruling was overturned in the 1950s.)

In essence, this landmark Supreme Court Decision found censorship to be constitutional.[20] Thus, the *Mutual vs. Ohio* Supreme Court Decision reinforced claims of motion picture critics and censors and opened the door for American film censorship, even Federal screen censorship. This decision not only created a favourable legal climate for film censorship in the United States, emboldening state and local censor boards, but also precipitated a growing fear of government intrusion in the motion picture industry and led to a necessary response to criticism by studios and filmmakers.

Director Allan Dwan recalled censorship 'from the beginning' during the silent film era. 'And then organizations were formed. We couldn't open a picture anywhere without passing four or five groups of censors. We'd have the town police first and then individual groups. They'd all be in our hair. And every little teeny thing was censorable.' He admitted, 'It was like a Sunday-school business in those days. But I think it stimulated us into inventing something that would get by and be decent. We made cleaner pictures, but maybe better pictures. I don't know anything sexier than the stuff [Rudolph] Valentino used to do and yet it was done with a suggestiveness that wasn't dirty.'[21]

By 1921, 36 states were considering film censorship legislation and many believed federal censorship was inevitable. The National Association of the Motion Picture Industry trade organization tried to deter state and local censor boards from restricting the content of films. By February, *Variety* reported Famous Players-Lasky (later, Paramount) studio 'Banned Sex Films... Crime and Underworld Stuff Allowable When It Serves a Moral Purpose—Illicit Love Forbidden', adopting a Fourteen-Point 'production code' of voluntary self-regulation that 'laid down the law' regarding 'sex'. 'For the first time in its history a "production code" has been issued...The object is to eliminate all matter which might come into the category as being "offensive".'[22] (See Box 1.)

Jesse Lasky's 1921 Fourteen-Point draft of a 'production code' list was influential, anticipating and bearing a striking resemblance to the later 1927 'Don'ts and Be Carefuls' and the Motion Picture Production Code of 1930.[38] By March, the National Association of the Motion Picture Industry published 'Thirteen Points', a set of guidelines for preliminary industry self-regulation, in an effort to discourage state/local censorship.[39] Nonetheless, the State of New York launched the Motion Picture Commission censorship review board. The Federal Trade Commission and Senate Judiciary Committee were also looking into investigating the American movie industry and monopolistic vertical integration of studios in the 1920s.[40]

Will Hays and Motion Picture Producers and Distributors of America

During the freewheeling 'Roaring 1920s' 'Jazz Age' of Prohibition speak-easies, bootlegging and revelry—and racy 'pre-Code' screen content—a series of high-profile motion picture industry scandals involving famous

Lasky's Fourteen Points[23]

1. No pictures showing sex attraction in a suggestive or improper manner will be presented.[24]
2. Pictures dealing with 'white slavery' will not be presented.[25]
3. Stories having as their basic theme an illicit love affair will be produced only if they convey a moral lesson.[26]
4. Nakedness will be banned.[27]
5. Inciting dances will be eliminated.[28]
6. Unnecessarily prolonged passionate love scenes will not be shown.[29]
7. Stories predominately concerned with the underworld of vice and crime should not be produced.[30]
8. No picture should be shown which makes drunkenness or gambling attractive.[31]
9. No picture should be made which might instruct the morally feeble in the methods of committing crime.[32]
10. No story or incident should be presented on the screen which needlessly offends the holders of any religious belief.[33]
11. No incident showing a shocking disrespect for an object of religious belief will be presented.[34]
12. Suggestive comedy business will be eliminated.[35]
13. Unnecessary depiction of bloodshed is to be avoided.[36]
14. Salacious titles, stills and advertising must not be used.[37]

stars and directors, such as Fatty Arbuckle, William Desmond Taylor and Wallace Reid, led Hollywood studios to fear Federal censure of American films and fuelled arguments from screen critics insisting that Hollywood was a bad influence on cultural morality. Wary of direct government regulation of films, and in an effort to counteract bad publicity, public outrage and investigations, and avoid state, regional and federal censorship, the film industry established the Motion Picture Producers and Distributors of America (MPPDA) trade organization and hired Will Hays, a former Post-

Motion Picture Producers and Distributors of America (MPPDA) president Will Hays. (University of Southern California Regional History Collection)

master General, Presbyterian elder and campaign manager for US President Warren Harding, as MPPDA president to improve the image of Hollywood in 1922.[41]

Hays ran the MPPDA from 1922 until 1945. A skillful public relations person, Hays was a 'front-man' and face for the motion picture industry representing Hollywood's image in the political area. On behalf of studios, Hays promised a concerned public and government screen critics that there would be self-regulation of the Hollywood film industry, including morality clauses in studio contracts for casts and crews (such as creative screen talent, stars and directors) and that moral principles would be observed and upheld in motion pictures. However, for the most part, while endeavouring to improve Hollywood's public image, these early efforts by Hays and the film industry emulated a kind of publicity 'smoke screen' and there was no real change in Hollywood screen content during this early 'Roaring 1920s' era.[42] By 1924, *The Dramatic Life of Abraham Lincoln* was promoted as: 'A GREAT SMASHING ROMANCE BUILT TO THE SPEED OF EVERY FLAPPER IN DETROIT! It's a Collection of Heart Broadsides! A Wallop in Emotion!' [that's] 'GOING TO HAND EVERY MAIDEN IN DETROIT THE SHOCK OF HER SWEET YOUNG LIFE!'[43]

Film scholar John Trumpbour observes that Hays encountered a great deal of pressure from international censors to ban Hollywood scripts and motion picture scenes offensive to foreign nations. Moreover, a number of European nations imposed quotas designed to boost domestic film production over American film imports. Yet Hays had a keen ability and was accomplished at dealing with the American federal government, the US State Department and American Department of Commerce, to effectively maintain Hollywood's domination of film markets overseas.[44]

While Hays is typically considered more of an industry 'PR' entity rather than a stringent censor who personally regulated individual films, he was in fact actively involved in the censorship of screen adaptations as early

The Don'ts and Be Carefuls

Resolved, that those things which are included in the following list shall not appear in pictures produced by the members of this Association, irrespective of the manner in which they are treated:

Pointed profanity – by either title or lip – this includes the words 'God', 'Lord', 'Jesus', 'Christ' (unless they be used reverently in connection with proper religious ceremonies), 'hell', 'damn', 'Gawd' and every other profane and vulgar expression however it may be spelled;

Any licentious or suggestive nudity – in fact or in silhouette; and any lecherous or licentious notice thereof by other characters in the picture;

The illegal traffic in drugs;
Any inference of sex perversion;
White slavery;
Miscegenation (sex relationships between the white and black races);
Sex hygiene and venereal diseases;
Scenes of actual childbirth – in fact or in silhouette;
Children's sex organs;
Ridicule of the clergy;
Willful offense to any nation, race or creed;

And be it further resolved, that special care be exercised in the manner in which the following subjects are treated, to the end that vulgarity and suggestiveness may be eliminated and that good taste may be emphasized:

The use of the flag;

as 1924 in establishing 'The Formula', a preliminary form of censorship regulation, which banned salacious works from being adapted. In fact, by 1925 Hays proclaimed they had prevented 160 plays and books, valued at $2–3 million in screen rights, from being filmed.[45]

International relations (avoiding picturizing in an unfavorable light another country's religion, history, institutions, prominent people and citizenry);

Arson;

The use of firearms;

Theft, robbery, safe-cracking and dynamiting of trains, mines, buildings, etc. (having in mind the effect which a too-detailed description of these may have upon the moron);

Brutality and possible gruesomeness;

Technique of committing murder by whatever method;

Methods of smuggling;

Third-degree methods;

Actual hangings or electrocutions as legal punishment for crime;

Sympathy for criminals;

Attitude toward public characters and institutions;

Sedition;

Apparent cruelty to children and animals;

Branding of people or animals;

The sale of women, or of a woman selling her virtue;

Rape or attempted rape;

First-night scenes;

Man and woman in bed together;

Deliberate seduction of girls;

The institution of marriage;

Surgical operations;

The use of drugs;

Titles or scenes having to do with law enforcement or law-enforcing officers;

Excessive or lustful kissing, particularly when one character or the other is a 'heavy'.[46]

'Don'ts and Be Carefuls'

A few years later, on the heels of 'The Formula', Hays initiated further efforts at Hollywood censorship by forming a committee including MGM's Irving Thalberg and other studio executives who began crafting the 'Don'ts and Be Carefuls' for screen content. In 1927 the MPPDA's 'Don'ts and Be Carefuls' provided guidelines for studio story departments regarding the selection and purchase of screen material for production with the aim of suggesting potential changes and cuts to films and seeking to help studios head off problems in pre-distribution; that is, before industry filmmakers produced and released a film. However, they did not have consistent enforcement nationwide regarding film production. Instead, these guidelines functioned in more of an advisory capacity and were an attempt to distill and avoid problem areas onscreen by outlining a list of objectionable film content (see Box 2).

Studio Relations Committee

In 1927, Hays also created the Studio Relations Committee (SRC), headed by former American Red Cross Executive Secretary Colonel Jason Joy (and later James Wingate, from 1932–33, who was also Director of Studio Relations of the American Motion Picture Producers [AMPP]), to oversee the implementation of the MPPDA's 'Don'ts and Be Carefuls' guidelines in Hollywood films.[47] The Studio Relations Committee's objective was to read scripts and point out potential problems. The SRC's role in endeavoring to censor or constrain objectionable film content was simply advisory at first, then it became obligatory to submit scripts for film production; the MPPDA began to monitor scripts in 1929. However, there was no enforcement mechanism to compel filmmakers or studios to follow SRC recommendations. Rather, the problem was left to local distribution offices to sort out. Further, a 'Hollywood jury' of producers and executives would frequently overturn SRC rulings in hopes of leniency for their films.

To make matters even more complicated, new problems arose with the film industry's conversion to sound after 1927, which required new writers for dialogue and generated more controversy in terms of film content and potential screen censorship as public criticism of the motion picture industry grew.

Motion Picture Production Code

By 1929, Hays took more substantial steps toward film censorship. He met with industry trade journal *Motion Picture Herald* editor/publisher and devout Catholic, Martin Quigley, in 1929 and proposed that they work with Jesuit priest, Father Daniel Lord, to put together a 'code' of cinematic conduct based on moral principles as they applied to mass entertainment. 'Silent smut had been bad,' Lord argued. 'Vocal smut cried to the censors for vengeance.'[48] Hays encouraged Quigley and Lord to write a draft of what would become the 'Motion Picture Production Code', which was adopted by the film industry in March 1930.

The Motion Picture Production Code of 1930, written by Lord, Quigley and industry executives, detailed twelve categories of 'repellent subjects', including restrictions on depicting crimes, sex, violence, vulgarity, obscenity, profanity, costume, dances, religion, location, national feelings, titles and other repellent subjects onscreen. Sexual issues, crime, violence and language were major concerns. Conceptually, the intrinsic assumption of the Production Code was based on the notion that screen entertainment had the potential to improve or degrade the screen viewing public's life. Thus, the Code outlined moral obligations for filmmakers. For example, it stipulated motion picture producers and directors should not confuse good and evil and were not (in theory) allowed to create films which led audiences to sympathise with bad characters or make negative actions look attractive. The Production Code functioned as a cinematic 'moral blueprint' adopted by the film industry in 1930; however, it was not fully enforced by Hollywood until mid-1934.

The Code included 'General Principles', which stipulated that:

1   No picture shall be produced which will lower the moral standards of those who see it. Hence the sympathy of the audience shall never be thrown to the side of crime, wrong-doing, evil or sin.
2   Correct standards of life, subject only to the requirements of drama and entertainment, shall be presented.
3   Law, natural or human, shall not be ridiculed, nor shall sympathy be created for its violation.[49]

The Code outlined a number of restrictions as 'Particular Applications' of general principles, specifically prohibiting:

- Nudity and suggestive dances.
- Ridicule of religion and ministers of religion, who were not allowed to be represented as villains or comic characters.
- Illegal drug use and the use of liquor 'when not required by the plot or for proper characterization'.
- Showing explicit methods of crime (e.g., smuggling, arson, safe-cracking, etc.) and glorification of illegal activity.
- Referring to alleged 'sex perversion' (e.g., the Code banned homo-sexuality, bisexuality and even interracial romance) and venereal disease, as well as showing childbirth. Portrayals of miscegenation were outlawed.
- Excessive brutality, violence and murder, which needed to be portrayed to discourage viewers from imitating violent behavior and killing in real life; screen brutality could not be shown in grisly detail.
- 'Revenge in modern times', which was not to be justified.
- Dishonouring the sanctity of marriage and the home, which had to be upheld.
- Depictions of adultery and illicit sex. 'Pictures shall not infer that low forms of sex relationship are the accepted or common thing.' While recognised as sometimes necessary to the cinematic plot, adulterous illicit sex was not supposed to be explicit or narratively justified onscreen and was not to be presented as an alluring acceptable opportunity.
- 'Scenes of Passion' which were discouraged when not essential to the plot. 'Excessive and lustful kissing' was to be avoided, along with any other suggestive screen treatment that might 'stimulate the lower and baser element'.
- Objectionable language; various words and phrases were banned and considered to be offensive.
- Disrespectful presentation of the United States flag, which was to be treated respectfully and people and history of other nations were to be presented 'fairly'.
- 'Vulgarity' or 'low, disgusting, unpleasant, though not necessarily evil, subjects' must be 'subject to the dictates of good taste'.
- Capital punishment, prostitution, 'third-degree methods', cruelty to children and animals; surgical operations must be delicately handled using sensitive care.[50]

Film historian Thomas Doherty describes Hollywood's Production Code as 'no mere list of Thou-Shalt-Nots but a homily that sought to yoke Catholic doctrine to Hollywood formula' where 'the guilty are punished, the virtuous rewarded, the authority of church and state is legitimate and the bonds of matrimony are sacred'.[51] The Production Code detailed an array of censorable film content to be avoided in Hollywood motion pictures and proscribed an extensive list of objectionable screen material.[52] (See Box 3.) The Code was later updated with minor revisions in 1938, 1939, 1946, 1947, 1951, 1954, then liberalised in 1956, on its last legs by 1966–1967 and finally abandoned in 1968. The Production Code made the moral and ethical case for censorial regulation of Hollywood films based on cinema's media-specific distinction from novels or plays, insisting movies be treated differently than literature in terms of censorship because of their mass appeal—thus, censors scrutinised screen adaptations, which filmmakers such as producer David O. Selznick found intrusive.[53] The Code also included 'Reasons Supporting the Preamble of the Code', which provides insight into what censors were thinking in their censorial reasoning for regulating films (see Appendix).

The Motion Picture Production Code[54]

Motion picture producers recognize the high trust and confidence which have been placed in them by the people of the world and which have made motion pictures a universal form of entertainment.

They recognize their responsibility to the public because of this trust and because entertainment and art are important influences in the life of a nation.

Hence, though regarding motion pictures primarily as entertainment without any explicit purpose of teaching or propaganda, they know that the motion picture within its own field of entertainment may be directly responsible for spiritual or moral progress, for higher types of social life and for much correct thinking.

During the rapid transition from silent to talking pictures they have realized the necessity and the opportunity of subscribing to a Code to govern the production of talking pictures and of re-acknowledging this responsibility.

On their part, they ask from the public and the public leaders a sympathetic understanding of their purposes and problems and a spirit of co-operation that will allow them the freedom and opportunity necessary to bring the motion picture to a still higher level of wholesome entertainment for all the people.

General Principles

1. No picture shall be produced that will lower the moral standards of those who see it. Hence the sympathy of the audience should never be thrown to the side of crime, wrongdoing, evil or sin.

2. Correct standards of life, subject only to the requirements of drama and entertainment, shall be presented.

3. Law, natural or human, shall not be ridiculed, nor shall sympathy be created for its violation.

Particular Applications

I. Crimes Against the Law

These shall never be presented in such a way as to throw sympathy with the crime as against law and justice or to inspire others with a desire for imitation.

1. Murder

a. The technique of murder must be presented in a way that will not inspire imitation.

b. Brutal killings are not to be presented in detail.

c. Revenge in modern times shall not be justified.

2. Methods of Crime should not be explicitly presented.

a. Theft, robbery, safe-cracking and dynamiting of trains, mines, buildings, etc., should not be detailed in method.

b. Arson must be subject to the same safeguards.

c. The use of firearms should be restricted to essentials.

d. Methods of smuggling should not be presented.

3. Illegal Drug Traffic must never be presented.

4. The Use of Liquor in American life, when not required by the plot or for proper characterization, will not be shown.

II. Sex

The sanctity of the institution of marriage and the home shall be upheld. Pictures shall not infer that low forms of sex relationship are the accepted or common thing.

1. Adultery, sometimes necessary plot material, must not be explicitly treated, or justified, or presented attractively.

2. Scenes of Passion

a. They should not be introduced when not essential to the plot.

b. Excessive and lustful kissing, lustful embraces, suggestive postures and gestures, are not to be shown.

c. In general passion should so be treated that these scenes do not stimulate the lower and baser element.

3. Seduction or Rape

a. They should never be more than suggested and only when essential for the plot and even then never shown by explicit method.

b. They are never the proper subject for comedy.

4. Sex Perversion or any inference to it is forbidden.

5. White Slavery shall not be treated.

6. Miscegenation (sex relationships between the white and black races) is forbidden.

7. Sex Hygiene and venereal diseases are not subjects for motion pictures.

8. Scenes of Actual Child Birth, in fact or in silhouette, are never to be presented.

9. Children's Sex Organs are never to be exposed.

III. Vulgarity

The treatment of low, disgusting, unpleasant, though not necessarily evil, subjects should be subject always to the dictate of good taste and a regard for the sensibilities of the audience.

IV. Obscenity

Obscenity in word, gesture, reference, song, joke, or by suggestion (even when likely to be understood only by part of the audience) is forbidden.

V. Profanity

Pointed profanity (this includes the words, God, Lord, Jesus, Christ — unless used reverently — Hell, S.O.B., damn, Gawd), or every other profane or vulgar expression however used, is forbidden.

VI. Costume

1. Complete nudity is never permitted. This includes nudity in fact or in silhouette, or any lecherous or licentious notice thereof by other characters in the picture.
2. Undressing Scenes should be avoided and never used save where essential to the plot.
3. Indecent or Undue Exposure is forbidden.
4. Dancing Costumes intended to permit undue exposure or indecent movements in the dance are forbidden.

VII. Dances

1. Dances suggesting or representing sexual actions or indecent passion are forbidden.
2. Dances which emphasize indecent movements are to be regarded as obscene.

VIII. Religion

1. No film or episode may throw ridicule on any religious faith.
2. Ministers of Religion in their character as ministers of religion should not be used as comic characters or as villains.
3. Ceremonies of any definite religion should be carefully and respectfully handled.

IX. Locations

The treatment of bedrooms must be governed by good taste and delicacy.

X. National Feelings

1. The Use of the Flag shall be consistently respectful.
2. The History, institutions, prominent people and citizenry of other nations shall be represented fairly.

XI. Titles

Salacious, indecent, or obscene titles shall not be used.

XII. Repellent Subjects

The following subjects must be treated within the careful limits of good taste:

1. Actual Hangings or electrocutions as legal punishments for crime.
2. Third Degree methods.
3. Brutality and possible gruesomeness.
4. Branding of people or animals.
5. Apparent Cruelty to children or animals.
6. The Sale of Women, or a woman selling her virtue.
7. Surgical Operations.[55]

Advertising Code

A June 1930 Code addendum included a film publicity 'Code of Motion Picture Advertising', known as the Advertising Code (see Box 4).

The Advertising Code was more lenient than the Production Code, as evident in racy studio advertising for pictures, typically more salacious than the actual films, although pre-Code films frequently violated the Code.

Pre-Code Period and Early Films

While the Production Code functioned as a cinematic 'moral blueprint', significantly there was no enforcement mechanism to compel Hollywood filmmakers to adhere to Code strictures. As the Great Depression struck in America following the 1929 stock market crash, economically hard-hit studios were desperate and needed to attract audiences and increase

Code of Motion Picture Advertising

1. We subscribe to the Code of Business Ethics of the International Advertising Association, based on 'truth, honesty and integrity'.
2. Good taste shall be the guiding rule of motion picture advertising.
3. Illustrations and text in advertising shall faithfully represent the pictures themselves.
4. No false or misleading statements shall be used directly or implied by type arrangements or by distorted quotations.
5. No text or illustration shall ridicule or tend to ridicule, any religion or religious faith: no illustration of a character in clerical garb shall be shown in any but a respectful manner.
6. The history, institutions and nationals of all countries shall be represented with fairness.
7. Profanity and vulgarity shall be avoided.
8. Pictorial and copy treatment of officers of the law shall not be of such a nature as to undermine their authority.
9. Specific details of crime, inciting imitation, shall not be used.
10. Motion picture advertisers shall bear in mind the provision of the production code that the use of liquor in American life shall be restricted to the necessities of characterization and plot.
11. Nudity with meretricious purposes and salacious postures, shall not be used.
12. Court actions relating to censoring of pictures, or other censorship disputes, are not to be capitalized in advertising.[56]

viewership during this lean, difficult time. Filmmakers met these challenges by using sex and violence as a vehicle to lure Depression audiences into theatres to see early sound-era films, referred to as 'pre-Code' films because they were quite salacious and censorable yet not rigidly subjected to the Code.

Despite myriad censorial efforts to restrict film content, paradoxically, cinema censorship was not yet strictly enforced. The 'pre-Code' period is a

Ten Code
Violations 'Thou
Shall Nots.'
(Academy of
Motion Picture Arts
and Sciences)

bit of a misnomer because it typically refers to films in the early sound-era between 1930 and 1934 when the Code existed but was, for all intents and purposes, ignored or loosely applied.[57] In fact, during this pre-Code period, film content was often in complete violation of the Production Code, as ample primary archival evidence on censorship from this period indicates. For instance, in August 1932, Hays complained about the 'objectionable trend' in censorable content that prevailed in Hollywood films, 'mistakes' made and the 'responsibility' of studios and stressed the necessity of the film industry's Production Code compliance. Hays observed 'several pictures... grossly violate the spirit and... letter of the Code... Studios endeavor to find ways to violate their own pledged obligation'.[58] He argued that free 'expression' is not lost in cleaning up the cinematic screen: 'Whenever motion picture production confesses that it cannot derive inspiration or material except from adultery, libertinage and illicit adventure, it will no longer deserve legislative tolerance or supporting patronage...the infection will start which will disease the industry itself and bring its disrepute.'[59] Hays maintained:

> Liberty of expression is not imperiled when protest is made against playwrights who glean their plots from the scribblings on latrine walls or search the garbage dumps and sewers of society for situations and characters. The great majority of the millions of folk in America refuse to be spattered with the spittle of decadent imaginations and will not bring themselves or families within range of that theater's ribald impudence which continues to prostitute all proprieties.[60]

'Make no mistake,' Hays insisted, 'multitudes... do not now patronize motion pictures because they are not convinced that the screen has been purged of erotic scenes and indecent expressions.'[61]

Mae West gives a 'Hot Time' to America in *She Done Him Wrong*. (Paramount, 1933)

Mae West invites
Cary Grant to come
see her in *She
Done Him Wrong*.
(Paramount, 1933)

Of course, plenty of 'erotic scenes' and 'indecent expressions' abounded
in motion pictures to give Hays reason for concern about early 1930s sound-
era pre-Code films, which included a vast assortment of censorable screen
material: from screen violence and gangland hoodlums in *Little Caesar*
(1930), murderous monsters in *Dracula* (1931) and *Frankenstein* (1931),
to nudity, sexual impropriety and lewd behavior in bawdy, adulterous
comedy. For instance, Mae West boldly looks Cary Grant up-and-down and
invites him to 'come up and see me sometime' and describes nude shots
of her in the bath as 'for the bedroom—a little spicy but not too raw' with
ample sexual innuendo in comedies such as *I'm No Angel* (1933) and *She
Done Him Wrong* (1933).

An abundance of nudity and naked women appear in African safari
Trader Horn (1931) and South Sea adventure *Bird of Paradise* (1932). Jean
Harlow's irreverent 'bad girl' bathes naked in a barrel outdoors in front of
Clark Gable in *Red Dust* (1932) and gleefully seduces affluent married men
while simultaneously having affairs with their chauffeurs in *Red Headed
Woman* (1932). In fact, Hays and Joy received angry letters from civic groups,
religious leaders and other studios complaining that Harlow's salacious
pre-Code *Red Headed Woman* film was approved by censors and released.

Other pre-Code films also pushed the envelope of screen censorship.
For example, Marlene Dietrich's *Blonde Venus* (1932) swims naked in a

lake, entices nightclub patrons as a seductive cabaret singer, has an affair, leaves her husband, poses as a prostitute in a flophouse, is forced to give up her young son, then runs off with wealthy playboy Cary Grant. Not surprisingly, the MPPDA rejected the original script for *Blonde Venus* written by director Joseph von Sternberg as 'utterly impossible' where unfaithful wife Helen (Dietrich) commits adultery, yet gives up her 'glamorous career on the stage in Paris' and her love affair 'engagement to a millionaire', Nick (Grant) while she was still married to return to her 'impoverished husband', Ned (Herbert Marshall) and son. Censors forced Sternberg (and Paramount) to rewrite the screenplay three times. The MPPDA took issue with the violation of Production Code provisions upholding the law and marriage where 'Law natural or human shall not be ridiculed, nor shall any sympathy be created for its violation' and the 'sanctity of the institution of marriage

Cabaret diva
Marlene Dietrich
entices nightclub
playboys in
Blonde Venus.
(Paramount, 1932)

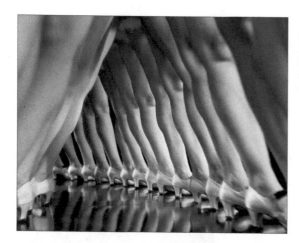

Busby Berkeley shot between the legs of showgirls in *42nd Street*. (Warner Bros., 1933)

and the home should be upheld'. Censors also insisted the film needed some kind of narrative moral retribution or 'compensating moral values' in the end. Paramount producer B. P. Schulberg drafted a second script, which was also rejected. Sternberg left the picture and tried to leave the studio when Paramount and censors interfered with his film, but was put on suspension and returned to revise the script a third time (reinstating much of the original version which censors approved after 'minor revisions') and finally shot the film—although some versions cut the opening scene where she swims naked.[62] Another film, *Tarzan and His Mate* (1934) featured a nude swim scene with a topless naked Jane (in three revealing versions: with a loincloth, bare breasts and a nude version) that was also cut by censors.

Busby Berkeley's sensational, provocative dance sequences showed tough guys brawling and prostitutes being roughed-up, stabbed to death, plunging out of windows, laying scantily-clad and drugged-up in opium dens and smoking suggestively under streetlamps lamenting the plight of homeless 'forgotten men' (returning veterans) living in tent camps, as the camera erotically looks up the skirts and between the legs of near-naked showgirls in *42nd Street* (1933), *Footlight Parade* (1933) and *Gold Diggers of 1933* (1933).

As films violated the Production Code in the salacious 'pre-Code' era, censors in 1932 were alarmed at the rising 20 per cent of films they called

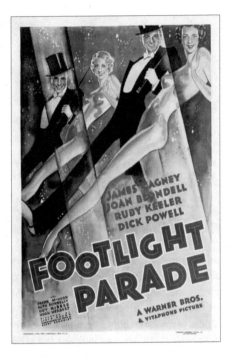

Publicity for *Footlight Parade*
was even racier than the movie.
(Warner Bros., 1933)

'sex pictures' dealing with 'illicit sex relations', 'prostitution', 'premarital affairs', 'kept women', 'pregnancy before marriage' and 'rape'.[63] Yet even in the more lenient pre-Code Prohibition era, the 'gruesome' and 'horrific' violent nature of horror pictures like *Frankenstein* (1931) and *Dracula* (1931) and gangster crime films about Al Capone, shocked censors who sought to ban horror and gangster films.[64]

Pre-Code Gangster Films and Scarface

In addition to sex and adultery providing scandalous screen material which violated the Production Code, provocative motion picture portrayals of illegal criminal activity and violence also challenged censors and flew in the face of the Code's strictures. In particular, gangster films, based on contemporary newsreels of real-life gangsters and pulp stories, were popular during Prohibition (1919–1933) and the Great Depression. These crime pictures revealed a corrupt 'urban jungle' in American cities and featured sadistic violence—misogyny, abuse of animals and brutality toward mob adversaries—with a tough milieu, gritty fast-paced style and shadowy 'look' to convey a seedy 'Jazz Age' atmosphere of sex, murder, speakeasies, booze, cabarets, prostitution and an American screen setting immersed in illegal activity. Crime pictures also rankled Code censors as films became more atmospheric and suggestive, as in Joseph Von Sternberg's acclaimed silent gangster yarn *Underworld* (1927) and moody *The Docks of New York* (1928), which Rudolph Arnheim considered 'uncannily lewd [in] detail' as a prostitute 'lustfully strokes' a sailor's 'naked arm with indecent tattoo marks all over it, as he ripples the muscles on it for her amusement... this woman sees nothing of the man but power, nudity, muscle'.[65] Needless to say, these films included a litany of censorable celluloid activities that would soon be banned by enforcement of the Code.

Notable pre-Code crime films included Warner Bros. pictures such as Mervin Leroy's *Little Caesar* (1930, with Edward G. Robinson), William Wellman's *Public Enemy* (1931, where hoodlum James Cagney is seduced by Jean Harlow, kills a horse, knocks off rival hoodlums and smashes a grapefruit in Mae Clark's face) and LeRoy's powerful 'social problem' film, *I Am a Fugitive from a Chain Gang* (1932). In fact, Warner Bros. production chief Darryl Zanuck championed hard-edged social realism during this early-1930s pre-Code period. For instance, in a January 1931 letter to the MPPDA's Jason Joy, Zanuck defended gangster pictures like *Public Enemy* and pulp fiction like Dashiell Hammett's hard-boiled detective story *The*

Public Enemy
James Cagney
smashes a
grapefruit in
Mae Clark's face.
(Warner Bros.,
1931)

31

Maltese Falcon as offering social critique of a growing urban American crime problem that did not therefore violate the Production Code. He argued: 'Prohibition did not cause crime, gang violence, or a corrupt environment, but rather Prohibition merely served to bring crime before the public eye.'[66]

Thus, while Warner Bros.' spicy pre-Code 1931 version of Dashiell Hammett's hard-boiled detective tale, *The Maltese Falcon*, featured 'taboo' illicit sexual connotation and the private eye's mistress accusing him of infidelity with the saucy line, 'Who is that dame wearing my kimono?', it was nonetheless approved by censors. However, the sympathetic portrayal of crime, violence and Paul Muni's Al Capone-like gangster *Scarface* (1932) caused quite a stir and faced a slew of censorship problems. 'Screw the Hays Office!' producer Howard Hughes declared. 'Make it as realistic and grisly as possible.' *Scarface* was controversial to the Hays Office because it seemed to condone illegal Prohibition-era crime and criminals and suggested the gangster 'Scarface' Tony Camonte (Paul Muni) had an incestuous relationship his sister Cesca (Ann Dvorak).

In particular, censors affected the production of *Scarface* as Hays intervened to force Hughes and director Howard Hawks to change scenes, tone down violence, present the mobster as weak and cowardly, add the subtitle 'The Shame of the Nation', add a disclaimer about the problem of gangster crime violence in America, not glorify violence and criminal activity, shoot a different ending and effectively delay its release for a year. When asked why *Scarface* was made in 1930 but not released until 1932, Hawks replied: 'Censors. Hughes was fighting them. He'd fight anybody. Hughes wouldn't do what they wanted to do. I think the censors, in their stupid way, said that anybody who commits things like Scarface did had to pay for it. You had to show them. We fought them for about a year and finally ended up making what they wanted us to make.' Hawks admitted: 'There were a lot of things I never saw. They made a lot of strange scenes. I didn't have anything to do with the scenes with the mayor of the city.'[67]

Yet, liberties taken with the Code for *Scarface*, with the justification that it was drawn from real-life gangsters, did not go unnoticed. As a result, there was much criticism directed toward Hays, the studios and the MPPDA. *Scarface* also illustrated that state and local censorship boards, a thorn in the side of studios, could affect production to cut and reshoot a film for a particular state. For example, *Scarface* was shown with different endings in New Jersey versus New York. One version depicted Muni shot down by

Scarface Paul Muni's Al Capone gangster fires his Tommy Gun and laughs at the cops. (Caddo Co., 1932)

police in a shower of Tommy machine gunfire, while in an alternate version other states and local viewers (and censors) wanted to see cinematic depictions of the legal apparatus working, functioning to ensure justice, with a moralising conclusion that showed the gangster being hanged in an execution at the end. Yet, despite the fact that the supposed glorification of gangster violence in *Scarface* caused a stir with Hays, state censors and the MPPDA, censors would not fully enforce the Production Code in Hollywood films until a few years later, in mid-1934.

2   ENFORCING THE MOTION PICTURE PRODUCTION CODE

Notably, at the height of Hollywood screen censorship in the mid-1930s into the wartime era of the 1940s, there were several different layers of cinematic censorship to which films were subject in a complex labyrinth of censorial regulation and screen constraints: Hollywood's official MPPDA 'Hays Office' Production Code Administration (PCA) film industry self-regulation which ultimately enforced its moral 'Code' censorship; a litany of different US state and local censorship boards, resistance and ratings scrutiny leading to threatened boycotts of 'condemned' films by numerous religious organisations such as the National Catholic Legion of Decency; the federal government regulation of wartime films by the Office of War Information (OWI) to further propaganda aims during World War II; and an array of international censorship agencies in different nations for exporting films overseas.

The MPPDA's 'Hays Office' efforts at fostering cinematic decency on Hollywood screens did encounter a few critics. By 1935, film star Marlene Dietrich criticised the Production Code and insisted, 'Censorship is idiotic and inconsistent. Hollywood pictures today are not helped by it. The Hays Office cuts out legs but keeps in innuendos that are far worse.'[68] Hard-boiled crime fiction writer James M. Cain complained, 'I think the whole system of Hays censorship, with its effort to establish a list of rules on how to be decent is nonsensical'. He added: 'A studio can obey every one and be salacious—violate them and be decent.'[69] Cain had reason to be upset.

He had the misfortune of pitching his spicy 'red meat' story, *The Postman Always Rings Twice*, a sexy, adulterous murder yarn, to Hollywood studios at the worst possible time: as the National Catholic Legion of Decency launched a major effort against American studios and threatened to boycott unsavoury, improper films in spring 1934.

As a result, despite studios' initial interest in Cain's racy novel, Hays (and 'shocked' MPPDA censor Joseph Breen) intervened and discouraged Hollywood studios from adapting it because it violated the Production Code. MGM had even purchased the screen rights in March 1934, but Hays insisted it was a 'salacious', 'dangerous' 'deception' that was 'impossible' to film and condemned the project in an eight-page denunciation.[70] Thus, censors effectively banned *The Postman Always Rings Twice* from being produced for a decade.

Censors justified scrutinising motion pictures as protecting children, parents and families. From 1929–1932, Payne Fund Studies scientific research investigated the influence of films on American youth, concluding Hollywood's strong impression undermined parental-, school- and church-teachings. Yet, censors endeavoured to regulate films aimed at adults and children.[71] American screen censors further restricted Hollywood film content in response to myriad pressures by 1934, as civic and religious groups such as the Legion of Decency campaigned, denounced and threatened to boycott 'immoral' films.

The Legion of Decency

Coinciding with increasing pressure to censor motion pictures, the Catholic Church mounted an offensive against Hollywood beginning in 1933 and formed the Legion of Decency. By April 1934, the Legion of Decency pledged to boycott and blacklist films with 'morally offensive' content labeled 'indecent' by the church as vile, unwholesome and a grave menace to corrupt society. The Legion was a powerful force to be reckoned with during this period, with between 11 and 22 million members at its peak. Other religious organisations rallied behind the Legion's efforts.

On December 11, 1935, Hollywood trade paper *Variety* announced in bold headlines 'CHURCH TIGHTENS ON PIX' and reported on the Legion of Decency's three grades and classifications for films, an alliance between Episcopalians and Catholics to crack down on 'backsliding' salacious motion picture screen content, the organization's hint of boycotts on films and theatres, their proclaimed support for new Legion ratings of 'not disapproved', 'disapproved for children' and 'disapproved for all' for future films and printed a Legion pledge to not see indecent, condemned films.[72]

By 1936, the Legion had published its ratings system:

A – Suitable for all
B – Morally objectionable or unsatisfactory in part for all
    (neither recommended nor condemned)
C – Condemned

The A rating was eventually expanded to include:
A–I – Suitable for all audiences
A–II – Suitable for adults (later changed to 'Suitable for adults and adolescents')

It was later revised and expanded in 1957 to add:[73]
A–III – Suitable for adults only.

A few years later, by 1962–63, it was further expanded to include:
A–IV – For adults with reservations

(There was also a rarely used Separate Classification 'S.C.' rating, a special category given to certain films the Legion criticised but did not outright condemn, which ultimately became A-4. Decades later, in 1978, the B and C ratings were combined into a new O rating for 'morally offensive' films. The Legion of Decency changed its name to the National Catholic Office for Motion Pictures [NCOMP] on July 8, 1965.)

The Legion of Decency had members recite an annual pledge against seeing what they considered to be 'unwholesome', 'salacious' films. The 1933 version read:

I wish to join the Legion of Decency, which condemns vile and unwholesome moving pictures. I unite with all who protest against them as a grave menace to youth, to home life, to country and to religion. I condemn absolutely those salacious motion pictures which, with other degrading agencies, are corrupting public morals and promoting a sex mania in our land... Considering these evils, I hereby promise to remain away from all motion pictures except those which do not offend decency and Christian morality.

In 1934, the pledge was updated to insist that the nation's Catholic Legion members boycott all 'indecent' and 'immoral' banned films and the theatres that showed them:

I condemn all indecent and immoral motion pictures and those which glorify crime or criminals. I promise to do all that I can to strengthen public opinion against the production of indecent and immoral films and to unite with all who protest against them. I acknowledge my obligation to form a right conscience about pictures that are dangerous to my moral life. I pledge myself to remain away from them. I promise, further, to stay away altogether from places of amusement which show them as a matter of policy.[74]

Studios realised the Legion was a formidable opponent, as it threatened film boycotts amid the challenging economic climate of the lean Depression years and that the industry therefore needed to take action and respond. The Legion was a massive threat during a crucial time as several Hollywood studios had gone into receivership and sought an economic comeback. Further, US Representative Wright Patman had even attempted to form a national body of Federal censorship to inspect films, the Federal Motion Picture Commission, in congressional hearings.

Joseph Breen and the Production Code Administration 'Hays Office'

In response to concerns about the possibility of outside government censorship of the film industry, Hollywood studios established the Production Code Administration (PCA) or 'Hays Office' as an industry self-censoring regulatory body within the MPPDA in July 1934 (operational by August 1934) and hired Joseph Breen, a Catholic and former journalist who had worked with Hays as a troubleshooter at the MPPDA since 1931, as chief censor to enforce the Production Code and run the PCA. As America's film censor, Breen applied the Code to Hollywood films from 1934 until his retirement from the PCA in 1954. As the Production Code was finally going

Production Code Administration (PCA) 'Hays Office' chief censor Joseph Breen. (University of Southern California Regional History Collection)

to be more strictly enforced, on August 11, 1934, *Motion Picture Herald* reprinted the Production Code with the headline: 'What the Production Code Really Means.'[75]

In practice, Breen and the PCA enforced the Code to placate censors and critics of the film industry. In particular, Breen and Production Code Administration censors examined all materials (including scripts, costumes and song lyrics), passed judgment as to whether the film was acceptable (or unacceptable) to the Production Code and examined and evaluated the finished motion picture production. A PCA Seal of approval was issued to final film productions that passed, or a list of any any changes needed to comply with the Code was provided.

Code censorship was enforced by the film industry in a system of self-regulation whereby the 'Big Five' vertically-integrated major Hollywood studios (MGM, Paramount, Twentieth Century-Fox, Warner Bros. and RKO) agreed not to screen films without a PCA Seal of approval in their first-run theatres and imposed a $25,000 fine on studios or filmmakers if a film was released without a PCA Seal. This was self-censorship on the part of the studios which controlled the industry's production, distribution and exhibition and owned 77% of the lucrative first-run motion picture theatres in major urban areas across the US.[76] In addition, the 'Little Three' major-minor studios (Columbia, Universal and United Artists) made deals with the Big Five to also abide by the Code in order to be able to release their films into major theatres.

Thus, Hollywood film censors significantly influenced screen content as they enforced the Production Code by mid-1934. 'The English trade paper *Film Weekly* called Hays "a mere Hindenberg", reserving for Joseph Breen the title "the Hitler of Hollywood"' in 1935, as film scholars Leonard Leff and Jerold Simmons observe. 'He cashiered properties, rewrote screenplays, supervised directors and edited films.' As they suggest, 'The Code was the Word, the gospel according to Breen'. Indicating his power in Hollywood during this mid-1930s period, Breen claimed to Will Hays, 'The responsible heads of the studios are a cowardly lot'.[77]

Breen required all Hollywood films to have 'Compensating Moral Values' and would negotiate with filmmakers and studios over film content. He insisted that a film could still show 'evil' acts as long as they were balanced within the narrative with compensating moral punishment and retribution for screen crimes, as well as reformation and repudiation of evil deeds (unlike earlier pre-Code films such as *Trouble in Paradise* in 1932). Breen's Compensating Moral Values requirement ensured that cinematic criminals were brought to justice and apprehended, either killed or sent to prison for their crimes, as seen in many gangster and film noir crime pictures. Thus, Breen and the PCA 'Hays Office' enforced Production Code censorship, which became a codified system of motion picture industry self-regulation that would affect Hollywood filmmaking through the 1950s. This more rigorous Code enforcement by the PCA was especially seen in the mid-1930s and would continue until Breen's retirement in 1954, before gradually becoming more lax and eventually declining in the 1960s.

The PCA also retroactively banned many pre-Code films from release. In 1935, the MPPDA ruled that any film released prior to July 15, 1934 that is reissued by studios must be submitted to and approved by the PCA. Thus, in 1935–36 Breen rejected the reissue of pre-Code films like racy Mae West comedies *She Done Him Wrong* and *I'm No Angel*, Berkeley musical *Footlight Parade*, gangster films *Public Enemy* and *Scarface*, 1931 versions of *The Maltese Falcon* and *The Front Page* and 1932 musical romance *Cock of the Air*. There was opposition from the PCA, local censors and other civic, religious and media groups regarding new Mae West comedies, culminating in a 'box-office poison' campaign against her and other strong independent female stars such as Dietrich and Katharine Hepburn in the 1930s.

In 1935, Breen and the PCA expressed concern regarding Mae West's *Klondike Annie* (1936), about a promiscuous 'Doll' who masquerades as a religious missionary saving souls while on the run for killing her Chinese lover. Censors objected to its representation of interracial sex violating the Code's miscegenation clause,[78] torture, the brazen sexual behavior and morality of West portraying a prostitute and murder that goes unpunished without compensating moral values. In July, Hays cautioned, 'We assume that there will be no suspicion of loose or illicit sex relationships between Miss West and the Chinese gambler or any of the characters in your story'. By the fall, Breen insisted on changes to West's script, scrutinised her risqué costumes, nixed suggestive camera shots and framing and eliminated lewd song lyrics. Censors cut a torture scene and a murder scene where West stabs her Chinese lover in self-defence and Breen removed sexually evocative content such as West's lines, 'Men are at their best when women are at their worst' and 'I'm sorry I can't see you in private' while she seductively eyes a handsome police officer from head to toe to look him over. However, West's saucy line in deciding between two lovers, 'When I'm caught between two evils, I generally like to take the one I never tried', remained in the film. *Klondike Annie* received a PCA Seal on December 31, 1935, yet Hays took particular issue with West playing a 'religious worker'. He admitted, 'My worst worry is not the alleged salaciousness, but is in the producer's failure to avoid the impression that it is a *mission* house picture and that "The Doll" was masquerading as a missionary'.[79] In February 1936, Breen discovered Paramount was previewing unedited versions of the film which had not been approved by the PCA and pulled the film's seal until the studio deleted suggestion of an 'illicit love affair' and sexual 'love talk' before approving it for release. The Legion of Decency, Hearst newspapers and Paul Block papers lobbied against the picture and it was banned in Australia. By May 1936, the San Francisco Motion Picture Council complained that the film's presentation of West's 'heroine as a mistress to an Oriental, then as a murderess, then as a cheap imitator of a missionary—jazzing religion—is not in harmony with other education forces of our social set-up. And these elements are particularly objectionable when they are interspersed with smutty wise-cracks.'[80] Years later, director George Cukor considered Mae West's suggestive humour with admiration and observed, 'there's a great deal of delicacy in what she does: I think it's all *inference*. Instead of laying it on the line, she was completely dressed.'[81]

Eventually, as Breen and the Production Code Administration cracked down on motion picture content, many Hollywood film genres transformed in response to the more stringent PCA constraints. Spicy promiscuous content in pre-Code genres such as sexually explicit comedies, women's pictures, 'fallen women' films or tales of wealthy playboys' mistresses, as in *Blonde Venus*, were toned down and sanitised and given a tamer domestic focus of mother-daughter relationships or romance. Screen humour and musical comedy changed from physical bawdy slapstick antics, the naughty sexual innuendo of Mae West, Jean Harlow and scantily-clad attire of pre-Code Berkeley musicals to the sophisticated verbal wit, fully-clothed wardrobes and twin beds where couples slept separately or kept one foot on the ground in sound-era screwball comedies such as *It Happened One Night* (1934), *Holiday* (1938), *His Girl Friday* (1940) and *The Philadelphia Story* (1940) and the ball gowns and tuxedos of Fred Astaire and Ginger Rogers musical comedies such as *Top Hat* (1935). As a result of Breen's more vigorous enforcement of the Code, the PCA deflated outside critics of the film industry, as strong opposition from the Legion, as well as state and local censorship boards, eased and finally faded: the Legion in due time relaxed its militancy and state/local censor boards became locales for political appointment, except in the South, where racial issues continued to result in ethnic or racial sequences being cut from films.[82]

However, in September 1935 independent producer David O. Selznick outlined the challenges filmmakers faced when taking on censorable subject matter, even in adapting acclaimed literary properties and having to submit screen material for PCA approval and adhere to the constraints of the Production Code and the Legion of Decency. In endeavoring to adapt Leo Tolstoy's novel *Anna Karenina*, for example, the 'problem was that of meeting censorship questions', Selznick explained, 'complicated by the fact that we undertook the production of the story at a time when the Legion of Decency's outcry was the loudest—that period when producers who attempted worthy pictures began to suffer for the sins of those who had stooped to a tasteless commercialism'. He added: 'It was further complicated by the new code that was drawn up by the producers, which had a blanket prohibition against stories dealing with adultery. Although it was conceded by authorities that there might be exceptions, yet it was made perfectly clear that the lesson was always to be taught that "adultery doesn't pay "... Our first blow was a flat refusal by the Hays office to permit the entire section of the story dealing with Anna's illegitimate child. This decision was so heartrending, especially as it meant the elimination of the marvelous bedside scenes between Anna, her husband and her lover, that we were sorely tempted to abandon the whole project.' Thus, as a result of comparatively stringent censorial constraints in the mid-1930s, 'we had to eliminate everything that could even remotely be classified as a passionate love scene'.[83]

Hollywood's Production Code censorship was also influential with film producers and distributors overseas. In April 1935, Gaumont-British studio chief Michael Balcon came to the US to ink distribution deals to release his British films in America and consulted with the PCA to learn more about Hollywood's Production Code to make certain that Gaumont-British pictures, such as Alfred Hitchcock's *The 39 Steps* (1935), did not violate—or encounter problems from—the Code. After his meeting with PCA officials, Balcon reported, 'I was very much impressed by my talks with Will H. Hays and Joseph I. Breen, Production Code Administrator, while I was in Hollywood. They explained the machinery to me and I became convinced of its practicability. After all, the code is in work here; pictures made in Hollywood and under it have improved. If we in England want distribution in this market, it is entirely logical that we should be prepared to observe the code principles.'[84] Yet, by May 16, 1935 *Motion Picture Daily* reported: 'British Take Critical View of Code Talks' with 'Some Editors Satirical On US Film Morals' as American Hays Office officials Martin Quigley and Carl Milliken went to Britain to explain US censorship and the Hollywood Production Code Administration to the British Federation of Industries film section, noting criticism of 'American moral standards and censorship' and 'open resentment over restrictions placed on US showings' of British films such as *The Scarlet Pimpernel*. 'If Queen Victoria wore low-necked evening gowns—and she did—that made them all right for films and if King Charles wanted Nell Gwyn taken care of after his death—well, what about it?—it was history.' However, it added, 'If the British industry desired to make expensive pictures it would have to cater to the idiosyncrasies of the American market. Industry leaders regarded the conferences as the most important industry happenings since British producers decided to seek outlets in the American market.'[85]

Nevertheless, ultimately, the function of the PCA transformed from stricter censorship in the mid-1930s to a process of negotiation, evolving into a practice of 'give and take' compromise regarding Hollywood film content.[86] Studio filmmakers also learned to manipulate the PCA and negotiate with Breen for content they absolutely sought to retain in films. For example, often, censors would give in if the studio could convince them of the importance of the work, especially for prestigious literary adaptations, such as *Camille* (1936), *Gone With the Wind* (1939), *Pride and Prejudice* (1940) and *The Grapes of Wrath* (1940). Moreover, screenwriters would pack scripts with outrageous censorable content in order to negotiate with the PCA for what they really wanted to include onscreen, in exchange for agreeing to cut obviously unsuitable material. Filmmakers could bargain for cinematic inclusion on the basis of artistic merit as Breen and PCA staff were nervous about being portrayed as philistines against the artistic development of the medium. Thus, Breen made deals with filmmakers, such as allowing Selznick to include the word 'damn' in *Gone With the Wind* by amending the profanity and vulgarity section of the Code on November 1, 1939.[87] Breen insisted Selznick eliminate the novel's racial slurs, Ku Klux Klan references and tone down excessive violence, childbirth, brothel and rape scenes for the film. Breen also permitted John Ford to depict prostitution in Claire Trevor's 'fallen woman' character Dallas, who is ridiculed and driven out of town in *Stagecoach* (1939).

Yet, Selznick, an independent producer, took issue with PCA censors' interference when he produced—with Alfred Hitchcock directing—Daphne de Maurier's '*roman noir*' Gothic romance novel, *Rebecca*. 'I think we have the ideal case to secure United Artists' support to telling the Hayes Association that we want no part of them or their code', Selznick asserted on September 6, 1939, in a direct challenge to the entire Production Code system of film industry self-censorship enforced by an association of major studios, questioning its legality. 'As I see it, the only recourse they would have would be to instruct their theatres not to play our pictures—and it seems to me ... that if we made decent pictures that passed all authorities, including censor boards, it would be a combination in restraint of trade to stop us from making anything we saw fit.' Pointing out the absurdity of the PCA's censorial taboos, he added: 'Here is a story [*Rebecca*] that has appealed to Americans by the hundreds of thousands and even millions— that was one of the three or four most popular books of the last five years and that a family publication like the *Ladies' Home Journal* saw fit to reprint without fear it was anything immoral.'[88]

As World War II commenced with Germany invading Poland in September 1939, curtailing international film distribution, Selznick complained: 'The whole damned Code becomes doubly onerous now that we are in danger of losing our foreign market. It was bad enough trying to make pictures that would break even when we had a world market to play to and with many of our best possibilities ruled out by the Code. But now, when we need at least something like the freedom that newspapers and magazines and book publishers and the legitimate stage have, when we need this freedom desperately, to have the industry itself strangle us is something that would be tolerated only by this shortsighted industry.' Selznick concluded: 'The whole story of *Rebecca* is the story of a man who has murdered his wife and it now becomes the story of a man who buried a wife who was killed accidentally!'[89] By February 27, 1940, Selznick endeavored to assure de Maurier: 'I have tried to do the most faithful job possible on *Rebecca*... there is one drastic change that was forced on us by the Hayes office and that almost caused us to abandon the picture.' He admitted, 'I don't want her to think we are imbeciles when she sees ... Maxim [DeWinter (Laurence Olivier)] did not actually kill Rebecca ... The Hays Office did what the censors would have done anyway—and that is, reject a story in which the murderer goes free.'[90] Nevertheless, Rebecca haunts Manderley mansion

Mrs. Danvers (Judith Anderson) longs for her lesbian affair with dead lover *Rebecca*. (Selznick International Pictures, 1940)

and possesses inhabitant Mrs. Danvers (Judith Anderson), obsessively longing for her (censorable) lesbian affair with the deceased Mrs. DeWinter.

Selznick and Hitchcock were further frustrated that their original plan to make a film of the Titanic disaster had been nixed by international political concerns in 1938. British shipping interests insisted it would damage the British shipping industry if the ship was identified as British—because it would be a 'harrowing tale of grief and suffering' with women forcibly 'torn away from their husbands and children from fathers' while men drowned. They insisted it would 'be regarded as an exceedingly unfriendly act. It would undoubtedly lead to diplomatic representations.'[91] In this case, a film was not made due to censorship, which is ironic given the later success of films on the subject. Hollywood (and British) filmmakers refrained from making movies about the Titanic until the 1950s—eventually producing films in 1953, 1958, 1964 and, of course, a blockbuster film in 1997. However, Nazi Germany actually made a propaganda film about the Titanic in 1943, supervised by Joseph Goebbels, where the British were the villains and a fictitious German first-officer was the hero. But we can only imagine what a Hitchcock film about the Titanic would have been like, since Selznick's 1938 project was censored.

There was a determination by the PCA to control political content, which resulted in apparent apathy over geopolitical convictions. For example, when MGM purchased Robert Sherwood's 1936 Pultzer Prize winning anti-Fascist dramatic play *Idiot's Delight* against Breen's recommendation, the PCA stipulated that filmmakers not criticise Mussolini and wanted the script for the film adaptation to be inoffensive. Breen consulted with the Italian consul and insisted that the film needed distribution in other countries. Sherwood altered the script, cut out the Italian connection and set the film in an unnamed European city where the native language was Esperanto, to keep the anti-war theme but avoid the anti-Fascist sentiment. Yet, the film wasn't released until 1939 and was not shown in Italy anyway, so critics lambasted the changes from the original dramatic work.

Production Code censors would also invoke constraints of international censor boards from other countries in an effort to justify and enforce PCA restrictions on Hollywood films, as in the case of William Wyler's Bette Davis film, *The Letter* (1940), adapting W. Somerset Maugham's play. When Warner Bros. submitted the project for PCA consideration on April 18, 1938, Breen rejected it and replied, 'We could not, of course, approve a motion picture, based upon this story'. The Hays Office objected to the inclusion of adultery and miscegenation in an illicit interracial affair. 'When this picture was produced by Paramount, at its Long Island Studios in 1929, it caused a very considerable nation-wide protest,' Breen declared. 'It was rejected, in toto, in England, in Canada and in Australia and the company had much difficulty in securing permission to exhibit it in a number of other foreign countries ... The British objection seems to hinge upon the characterization of the several British people, engaged in an illicit sex relationship and, more importantly, in the suggestion that... the murdered man, maintained a China woman as his mistress.' Breen concluded: 'We have no reason to believe that the official attitude throughout the British Empire will be any different now, than it was in 1929 and 1930.'[92] The studio eventually circumvented this Code restriction by changing the character to make it a Eurasian mistress and avoid further hassles. In modifying the story, associate producer Robert Lord asserted to executive producer Hal Wallis on December 20, 1939, 'In this treatment, I will try a scheme which I believe will enable us to get by the censors. I do not guarantee that we will get by, but it is certainly worth trying, because, in my opinion, if we can follow the play very closely and manage to get by the censors, we will have one of the most powerful and different motion pictures ever made.'[93] International censor boards were mentioned again to justify Code restrictions a few years later when Warner Bros. submitted *Kings Row* for PCA approval on April 22, 1941 and Breen remarked, 'You will have in mind, also, I am sure, that a picture of this kind could not be released in Britain, where *any* suggestion of insanity is always *entirely eliminated* from films'.[94] Other motion picture genres challenged the Code with cinematic crime, social realism and screen propaganda and eventually transformed and evolved in response to PCA censorship.

Transforming Crime Films: Gangsters, Social Realism and Espionage

In the 1930s, after the Great War, Prohibition, the Jazz Age, the Great Depression and the new Production Code, Hollywood censors tried to crack down on unsavoury film content and heralded a new era, moving from 'rawness to romance', insisting there needed to be fewer gangster and crime films. Hays opined, 'The greatest of all censors—the American public' was tired of '"hard-boiled" realism' in literature and stage.

He insisted America was done with its 'post-war preoccupation' with 'morbidity', 'crime' and 'orgy of self-revelation' in literature and drama as a 'new younger generation, now rising from the jazz age... promises to support clean high-purposed entertainment. The motion picture screen in recent months has done much to debunk the American gangster in films dealing with current crime conditions.' Hays added: 'Nothing could prove more forcibly the success of self-regulation in the motion picture industry than the manner in which such subjects have been invariably handled. The insistent message flashed upon the screen has been: "You can't get away with it".' He explained, 'the deadly weapon of ridicule has been trained upon the gangster and his kind... that removed from the bandit and the gunman every shred of false heroism that might influence young people'. Hays decried that there were too many crime films as 'the American public is growing tired not only of gangster rule, but of gangster themes' in literature, stage and screen.[95]

By mid-1934, Breen's more rigorous PCA enforcement of the Production Code had indeed influenced and transformed Hollywood genre films. The effects of censorship on these motion pictures were especially evident in the evolution of crime films, such as gangster pictures, which shifted focus from hoodlums to crime fighters. In fact, seeking to avoid depictions of what Breen called an 'orgy of sadism', censors proclaimed a sweeping moratorium on violent gangster, hard-boiled crime, G-Men and horror films, objecting to their 'excessive gunplay', 'brutality', 'shooting and killing', 'reckless disregard of human life' and 'gruesomeness' considered 'very offensive'. Breen noted state and local censor boards in the US and abroad in Canada and Great Britain were 'becoming alarmed' at the 'increase in pictures showing gangsters in violent conflict with the police'. In a 1935 memo to Hays, Breen called for a moratorium on all pictures showing American gangsters and reiterated, 'In September 1931 you will recall that the Board here, by formal resolution, agreed to call a halt on what was then generally referred to as "gangster" films'.[96]

By the mid-1930s, film censorship by the Production Code Administration discouraged or banned Hollywood from adapting hard-boiled crime stories and diluted the sexual content and excessive violence in crime pictures. While tough guy heroes and corrupt urban settings dominated screens in early gangster films, once the PCA began enforcing censorship by late-1934, censors were more inclined to object to promiscuity, brutality and romantic

Moll Jean Harlow seduces tough guy *Public Enemy* James Cagney. (Warner Bros., 1931)

portrayals of gangsters involved in 'unsavory' illegal activity (such as labour racketeering and prostitution). The Hays Office also retroactively censored hoodlums in August 1936. For example, after the PCA Code crack down on gangsters, Breen rejected Warner Bros.' reissue of *Public Enemy*, which he insisted 'definitely falls into the category of gangster pictures, which the Association agreed to discontinue some time ago. In view of this fact, we naturally could not issue a [PCA] Certificate at this time authorizing its re-issue.'[97]

In response to these censorial constraints, screen gangsters changed their stripes. After *Public Enemy* had made Cagney a star as a notorious mobster in the pre-Code era, Warner Bros. recast him as a crime-fighting FBI enforcer of the law in William Keighley's *G-Men* (1935) and gangster-turned-cop Edward G. Robinson shifted from portraying an iconic Prohibition era Al

Capone in *Little Caesar* to a crime fighter who went undercover to break up the mob opposite tough-guy Humphrey Bogart in William Keighley's *Bullets or Ballots* (1936).

In light of a changing censorial, cultural and production climate, gangster/crime films were transformed into social problem 'message' pictures. However, even 'reformed' crime films faced censorship controversy. The PCA initially rejected *Angels with Dirty Faces* when Warner Bros. submitted it on January 19, 1938. Breen objected to its crime, kidnapping, cop killing, unpunished murder by a gangster, a strip poker game, machine guns, a criminal's bulletproof vest, grisly details of the killing and preparation for an execution. He added, 'It is important to avoid any flavor of making a hero and sympathetic character of a man who is at the same time shown to be a criminal, a murderer and a kidnapper'.[98] In reforming criminals and infusing compensating moral values into Michael Curtiz' *Angels With Dirty Faces* (1938), Cagney's former-gangster 'repeat-offender' ex-con redeemed himself by dying like a coward while going to the electric chair. In an effort to be a role model and not corrupt the 'Dead End' street kids, he showed that his tough gangster was not admirable—and revealed he had a conscience to his best friend-turned-priest (Pat O'Brien), who he did prison time for.

In other crime films, John Garfield's prizefighter was framed for murder in Busby Berkeley's *They Made Me A Criminal* (1939), World War I veterans

Cagney points his gun at friend-turned-priest Pat O'Brien in *Angels With Dirty Faces*. (Warner Bros., 1938)

adapted their combat skills and turned to a violent life of crime in W. S. Van Dyke's *They Gave Him a Gun* (1937) and in Raoul Walsh's *The Roaring Twenties* (1939), starring real-life World War I veteran Bogart, Cagney plays combat veteran and former-gangster/bootlegger Eddie Bartlett, who is gunned down and meets his demise—then is sadly recalled as a washed up vestige of the Prohibition era: 'He used to be a big shot.' The famous line seemed to suggest Warner Bros.' final 'swan song' bidding farewell to the studio's renowned gangster genre.[99]

Yet by 1938–39, despite bans on gangsters, horror and grisly 'hard-boiled' novels, censors grew alarmed at the increasing number of crime films and a rising array of 'crime-horror' pictures from 1934–39. In 1938, Hays Office censors cautioned, 'Crime and horror pictures have increased from previous 15% of total number of feature pictures clearing through

Tough guys Cagney and Bogart in 'typical gangster picture' *The Roaring Twenties.* (Warner Bros., 1939)

the Production Code Administration, to 23% of entire volume... no less than 138 "Crime and Horror" pictures'. On August 5, 1939 Breen informed Hays about the 'steady increase in number of pictures in the Crime-Horror category' since 1934, citing 70 Crime-Horror films made in 1934, 83 in 1935, 106 in 1936, 91 in 1937, 104 in 1938 – or 28% of all films dealing with crime. By September 6, 1939, Breen expressed 'fears' to Hays 'concerning crime and horror films. Since explaining to the producers the seriousness of the situation of crime and horror films, production of this type of film has increased by 35%.' He noted that as of August 31, 1939 'there are 87 films in production and 46 of them are classified as crime or horror films'.[100]

In particular, Breen criticised *The Roaring Twenties* which he called a 'typical gangster picture' and complained, 'Its basic story violates the industry's agreement... the leading characters are members of gangs of bootleggers who engage in high crime and finally wipe out one another after a vicious gang battle in which everybody is killed'. He observed: 'There is one scene in this picture in an Italian restaurant, in which 8 or 10 people are slaughtered, as part of a gang fight; at the end of the picture there is another intra-gang battle in which all the important characters of the story are killed, the main character dying on the steps of a church on Christmas Eve ... The story not only is definitely in conflict with the Agreement of the industry in 1931, to keep away from gangster pictures, but it also violates our Regulations for the treatment of Crime, in that it depicts "action suggestive of whole-sale slaughter of human beings...between warring factions of criminals."' Breen warned Hays, 'Crime films [are] now up to 53% of production' by September 1939.[101]

The violence in crime films and horror pictures were a concern for censors in the US and abroad in Britain, France, Canada, Jamaica, India and Dutch East Indies. The British Board of Film Censors (BBFC) even added a new category, 'H' for Horror or Horrific, to its classification of films.[102] Indeed, the 'horrific' criminal nature of these films was not of the typical Al Capone, *Frankenstein* or *Dracula* variety. By 1939, censors recognized this menacing propagation of screen criminality, and added a new picture to their long list of 'crime-horror' films: Hitchcock and Selznick's adaptation of du Maurier's 1938 Gothic novel *Rebecca*. On the heels of gangster yarn *The Roaring Twenties* (1939) and Hitchcock's British production *Jamaica Inn* (1939, UK), these 'crime-horror' pictures were a different sort altogether, churned out like hotcakes by the 1940s in films such as *Stranger on the*

Third Floor (1940), *Rebecca* (1940), *The Maltese Falcon* (1941), *Suspicion* (1941), *This Gun For Hire* (1942), and *Gaslight* (1940, UK; 1944, US). Breen noted: 'It is also interesting to note that none of the...pictures are actually "horror" pictures, as we understand that term (i.e. none of them are pictures like *Frankenstein*, *Dracula*, etc.) Because of the refusal of the British Board of Censors in London to approve, for exhibition in the British Isles, pictures classified as "horror" pictures, we seem to have discontinued the production of these, so-called "horror" pictures.'[103] As censors scrambled to deal with the resurgence of deviant hoodlums and cinematic mayhem, the crime trend would eventually proliferate with films *Phantom Lady, Double Indemnity, Laura, Murder, My Sweet,* and be termed Hollywood's 'Red Meat' 'crime and romance' cycle in 1944, soon to be called 'film noir' by French critics overseas in 1946.[104] The concept 'film noir' would take many years to permeate US discourse.

As international tensions escalated abroad in 1930s Europe, which would eventually lead to a global conflict, Hollywood crime films incorporated espionage narratives and documentaries reported on the real-life events on the ground overseas. In *Hollywood and Hitler, 1933–1939*, Thomas Doherty examines motion picture screen images of Hitler and the Nazis in relation to the nexus between Hollywood's PCA regulation and US propaganda imperatives in feature films and documentary newsreels. For the most part, newsreels were generally accorded greater censorial latitude by censors because they typically practiced 'moral restraint' (often avoiding controversial topics) in their journalistic news of the day coverage emulating the news reporting freedom of speech granted to the press.[105]

A fascinating example is the *March of Time* newsreel short, *Inside Nazi Germany* (1938), which escaped regulatory problems by the industry's PCA censors, but was banned from being shown in Chicago by the Chicago Board of Censors as a propaganda film denigrating a foreign nation, Nazi Germany and therefore violating the Neutrality Act in 1938.[106] (However, this local censorship caused such an uproar that the Chicago Board reversed their decision a few days later.) Things would get even more heated later that year leading into 1939. In fact, MPPDA memos from 1938 reveal industry censors deliberated over the 'question [which] has arisen as to how to deal with war-related films with ideological import' regarding 'a joint concern over "political" films', essentially laying the groundwork for political and ideological censorship regarding potential propaganda aims as global tensions escalated and the world—and America—evolved ever closer to war.

By July 1938, Martin Quigley proposed '"amplifying" the Production Code', vis-à-vis international events, to Hays: 'No motion picture shall be produced which shall advocate or create sympathy for political theories alien to and subversive of, American institutions, nor any picture which perverts or tends to pervert the... screen from its avowed purpose of entertainment to the function of political controversy [promoting] alien political philosophies.'[107] In the wake of the dust-up over *Inside Nazi Germany*, by November 17, 1938, *Film Daily* reported, 'Newsreels to Huddle on Nazi Outrages' and MPPDA memos confirmed industry plans to take concerted propaganda action in meetings held on November 19, 1938 regarding the representation of Nazi Germany in American newsreels.[108] Even Hollywood feature films were bolder by 1939.

Anatole Litvak's *Confessions of a Nazi Spy* (1939) for Warner Bros., based on an actual 1938 FBI spy case, featured a former gangster icon-turned-crime fighter on an espionage hunt for Nazi spies on US soil. It was no coincidence that by the late-1930s Jewish actor and anti-Nazi activist Edward G. Robinson was no longer playing a gangster but rather a federal agent hunting subversive totalitarian enemies in this film. Despite the PCA's aversion to political content in films, Warners had 'declared war' on Germany, previously closing its German operations overseas in 1934 and refusing to do business with the Nazis, then cast gangster star Robinson as an FBI G-man ferreting out Nazi spies in America as the war broke out in Europe.

Confessions of a Nazi Spy was influential in challenging Production Code censorship of and aversion to depicting political propaganda in favour of publicicing the growing Nazi menace. Warner Bros. faced staunch opposition to producing *Confessions of a Nazi Spy* from PCA censors, as well as the German Consul in Los Angeles (who complained to Breen), from other studios such as Paramount's foreign office in New York and German Bunds which filed lawsuits and tried to prevent the film from being made. When Warner submitted the project to the PCA, Breen replied in December 1938 that although the script was 'technically' within the provisions of the Code, 'It is our thought that [censorship] boards in a number of foreign countries will not be disposed to approve the exhibition of a picture of this kind'.[109]

By January 22, 1939, PCA official Karl Lischka protested, 'Are we ready to depart from the pleasant and profitable course of entertainment, to engage in propaganda, to produce screen portrayals arousing controversy, conflict, racial, religious and nationalistic antagonism and outright, horrible human hatred?' He claimed *Confessions of a Nazi Spy* violated the Code which required that 'the history, institutions, prominent people and citizenry of other nations shall be represented fairly'. In particular, Lischka and PCA censors took issue with the film denigrating Hitler and the Nazis. He insisted that 'To represent Hitler only as a screaming madman and a bloodthirsty persecutor and nothing else, is manifestly unfair, considering his phenomenal public career, his unchallenged political and social achievements and his position as head of the most important continental European power'. After praising Hitler and objecting to the film's depiction of the Nazis, the PCA rejected the project and stated that making the picture 'will be one of the most memorable, one of the most lamentable mistakes ever made by the industry'.[110]

The same day as the PCA's rejection, the film's intended star gave an interview to the *New York Times*. America's renowned 'menace to society' was no longer the gangster. 'The gangster pictures performed a great service,' *Little Caesar* star Edward G. Robinson insisted. 'They aroused the public's consciousness of a rank and reckless state of affairs as nothing else could have done... They were, I believe, largely responsible for the repeal of prohibition and consequent abolition of the big mobs.' But as world events evolved overseas and tensions escalated in 1939:

> Today we are in a war much more serious than we were in then. We've got to fight to preserve our rights. The world is faced with the menace of gangsters who are much more dangerous than any we have ever known. And there's no reason why the motion pictures shouldn't be used to combat them... the motion pictures could dwarf any League of Nations ever devised by man if they were allowed to use their full power. Films and the radio are the most immediate and powerful forces in the world for informing men and shaping public opinion.[111]

As the conflict escalated, fighting Nazis on Hollywood screens undermined and violated the PCA's restriction on negatively portraying other countries.

Another controversial crime picture that reformulated the gangster cycle and was problematic for the Code was Charles Vidor's *Blind Alley* (1939), wherein a gangster's (Chester Morris) psychotic criminal mind, corrupted by the city, is revealed in vivid style through reverse-exposure images of his recurring nightmares. MGM originally tried to adapt the play on which it was based, *Smoke Screen*, in 1935, but censors nixed the project and told the studio to 'dismiss it entirely from further consideration' because its gangster hero was 'thoroughly unacceptable', insisting the story violated the Code 'so bad... that it was irrevocably beyond its pale' especially 'the *suicide* of the gangster, as a means of escape from the consequences of his crimes'.[112] Because it depicted crime, suicide and psychotic insanity, *Blind Alley* was shelved for several years until Columbia filmed it in 1939, when the PCA advised against displaying weapons or showing crime details and warned that British censors would reject 'any material dealing with insane characters and the use of an asylum as a background'.[113]

PCA censors also discouraged the cinematic portrayal of insanity by Peter Lorre as the murderous psychopathic stranger in Boris Ingster's 1940 noir crime film *Stranger on the Third Floor* and added an addendum to the PCA seal: 'The British Board of Film Censors will delete scenes of Peter Lorre if they regard him as insane. Other political censor boards will probably delete the [psychological] scenes of the death march [nightmare] and of the death chamber and Ward being strapped in the electric chair.'[114]

Social realist variations on the gangster genre such as *Angels With Dirty Faces*, *The Roaring Twenties*, *Blind Alley*, *Confessions of a Nazi Spy*, *Stranger on the Third Floor* and *Brother Orchid* (1940) are notable examples of genre experimentation and reveal Hollywood's effort by studios to reformulate gangster crime films. For instance, Lloyd Bacon's Warner crime comedy *Brother Orchid*, parodied Warner Bros.' gangster cycle when hoodlum crime boss and rival Humphrey Bogart nearly kills off mobster and former crime boss Edward G. Robinson who barely escapes death, then is revived and reformed into a monk at the serene Monastery of the Little Brothers of the Flowers. (Little Caesar's conversion from a kingpin to a divine pacifist—resembling Friar Tuck—combines gangster-comedy and social drama seemingly accommodating PCA piety.) While *Brother Orchid* begins by paying homage to the gangster genre and casting some of Warner Bros.' famed crime stars (Robinson, Bogart), it soon descends into parody and light-hearted comedy tempered by social realism that seems to also draw on the studio's successful period adventure pictures (such as *The Adventures of Robin Hood*'s [1938] veiled anti-fascist social commentary) with Donald Crisp as the monk heading the monastery and literally reforming the gangster. *Brother Orchid* was described as a 'lively farce', where an ex-gangster 'becomes a resident in a monastery where all the brothers engage in floriculture. When an outside gangster begins to cut in on the humble brothers' modest trade in flowers, Mr. Robinson—or *Brother Orchid*—goes forth to handle the situation.'[115]

Escalation of events in the war would eventually mitigate against the PCA's aversion to political content in Hollywood films. The *New York Times* announced 'sensational news' when Robinson 'revealed' that 'Hitler himself will appear' in *Confessions of a Nazi Spy* about 'Nazi spy activities in America' with Robinson as a 'G-man who nabs them' and 'actual newsreel shots of Hitler' to 'give the illusion of actual proximity. Der Fuehrer might even be invited to pay dues to the Screen Actors Guild.'[116] *Confessions of a Nazi Spy* pushed the envelope of Code censorship—and anticipated later coverage of the war which would also collide with PCA constraints—as it showed Nazi rallies, images from Leni Riefenstahl's Nazi propaganda documentary *Triumph of the Will* (1935), shots of Hitler's marching troops invading Austria and Czechoslovakia and German Bund footage in America. However, by September 1941 in Washington, a US Senate subcommittee investigated and accused Hollywood and specifically films such as *Confessions of a Nazi Spy* and Charlie Chaplin's brilliant parody of Hitler, *The Great Dictator* (1941), of producing pro-war propaganda.[117]

Breen and The Outlaw *on the Brink of World War II*

World events and Hollywood film censorship had evolved by March 1941, when President Franklin Roosevelt signed the Lend-Lease Act for America to aid the war overseas and an exhausted Breen resigned from the PCA, burned out after battling with Howard Hughes over his salacious western, *The Outlaw* (released 1943). Breen departed the PCA to become studio vice-president overseeing production at RKO, *Variety* reporting that 'Hays Purity Coder Adamant on Resigning'.[118] Even after he left the PCA, Breen still sent out memos complaining about controversial films like *The Outlaw* and *The Maltese Falcon*, although the 1941 remake of *The Maltese Falcon* was much tamer than the racier pre-Code version ten years earlier and Breen went from censoring Alfred Hitchcock's *Suspicion* (1941) to deciding on how to promote the film (and which ending to use).

Hughes' *The Outlaw*, in particular, challenged the PCA and stretched the boundaries of industry self-regulation when it received a Code Seal of approval in June 1941. Originally directed by Howard Hawks, producer Howard Hughes took over filming, which had begun in 1940, and introduced a buxom 19-year-old Jane Russell. Breen claimed the picture violated the Production Code by suggesting an illicit sexual relationship and abundant 'hanky-panky' between a scantily-clad Rio (Russell), revealing ample cleavage, with Billy the Kid (Jack Buetel) and Doc Holliday (Walter Huston).

Breen complained about the countless shots of Russell's uncovered breasts in *The Outlaw*. In a December 1940 letter to Hughes, Breen objected to the film's sex, violence and lack of compensating moral values where the 'criminal goes unpunished', its 'illicit sex between Billy and Rio', 'trick marriage', 'undue brutality' and 'unnecessary killings'.[119] When Breen viewed the film in March 1941, he insisted to Hughes that it violated the Code and denied the film a PCA Seal. Breen objected to a racy bed scene where Rio rubs herself against Billy's body, 'illicit' sex relations between Rio, Doc and Billy and concluded:

> in my more than ten years of critical examination of motion pictures, I have never seen anything quite so unacceptable as the shots of the breasts of the character of Rio... Throughout almost half the picture the girl's breasts, which are quite large and prominent, are shockingly emphasized.[120]

When Breen denied the film a Seal, Hughes appealed the decision to the MPPDA board in New York, which upheld Breen's rejection and Hughes was given a list of necessary cuts (roughly 40 feet of film showing Russell's breasts). Hughes agreed and received a Seal for *The Outlaw* (as Breen left the PCA for RKO), but tried to submit unedited versions of the film to state censor boards, which rejected the film and demanded additional cuts. As Hughes was embroiled in censorship battles, Twentieth Century-Fox decided not to distribute the picture since the studio would face a $25,000 MPPDA fine for releasing it without a PCA Seal. Then, Hughes shelved *The Outlaw*—and filmmaking—for over a year, instead focusing on his airplane factory as the United States entered the war.

The Outlaw: 'How would you like to tussle with Russell?' (Hughes Productions, 1943)

The Outlaw was not released until February 1943. Hughes finally showed it in one theatre in San Francisco accompanied by unapproved advertising which implied sexual content—which even the more lenient Advertising Code found objectionable—on huge billboards with salacious taglines that clamored: 'How would you like to tussle with Russell?' *Variety* called it 'bosom art'. After the San Francisco Motion Picture Council objected to the 'very disgusting portrayal of the feminine star... on large billboards' and the public protested, police removed the billboards. The Legion of Decency condemned the film and criticized the PCA for approving a Seal.[121]

The Outlaw was pulled from distribution (after Hughes tried to circulate unedited versions before its New York release) and not shown again until 1946, when non-MPPDA member studio United Artists released the film with unapproved advertising. Breen revoked the Code Seal, but it took months to cut it from all copies of the film. It was the first major challenge to PCA authority as Hughes purposely attempted to generate controversy to create box-office demand for his censored picture.

Code enforcement eased over time, especially later in the 1940s and after Breen's retirement in the 1950s. Moreover, Breen's brief departure from the PCA to serve as executive vice president in charge of production at RKO studio from mid-1941 to 1942, allowed moviemakers more latitude in screen content during his absence and tempered his own attitude upon his return to the PCA. RKO released Orson Welles' *Citizen Kane* (1941), one of the greatest films ushering in modern cinema history and Hitchcock's *Suspicion*, when Breen was at the studio. In fact, Breen moved from censoring a brothel scene in *Citizen Kane* (which Welles shot in 1940, but was cut from the film), to serving as RKO executive overseeing its promotion and release in 1941. Yet, Welles was marginalised in the Hollywood industry and his film projects nearly 'censored' from being screened at all. Serious efforts were made to prevent the release of *Citizen Kane* and destroy the film negative. Further, by autumn 1941, Welles shot test footage for an unfinished project, *The Story of Jazz*, which he had planned to make with Duke Ellington, Louis Armstrong, Billie Holiday and Oskar Fischinger. However, World War II and an RKO studio regime change forestalled the venture. Welles' jazz film was never made, although he discussed it with Armstrong. Instead, Welles was sent to South America to make *It's All True* (1943) while *The Magnificent Ambersons* (1942) was drastically cut in his absence. Then Welles was fired by RKO as the new studio motto heralded 'Showmanship Instead of Genius'. Changes in the industry and at the PCA coincided with increasing tensions and conflicts related to world events and the war. For example, while the PCA had previously discouraged and seemed determined to avoid including political content in Hollywood films, developments during World War II and government propaganda aims ultimately contradicted PCA policy.

Federal Censorship and World War II Propaganda Efforts

Hollywood filmmaking and the industry's self-regulation and enforcement of Production Code censorship was complicated by an array of factors with the onset of World War II. After the December 7, 1941 Japanese attack on Pearl Harbor which drew America into the conflict, US President Franklin Roosevelt initiated Federal censorship and propaganda efforts via the government Office of War Information (OWI) Bureau of Motion Pictures and Office of Censorship. Roosevelt created the OWI in June 1942 and ordered director Elmer Davis to 'formulate and carry out, through the use of press, radio, motion picture and other facilities, information programs designed to facilitate the development of an informed and intelligent understanding, at home and abroad, of the status and progress of the war effort and of the war policies, activities and aims of the Government'.[122]

The Office of War Information media regulation in Hollywood was the 'most comprehensive and sustained government attempt to change the content of a mass medium in American history', according to film historians Clayton Koppes and Gregory Black in *Hollywood Goes to War*, who investigate the US federal government effort at censoring the film industry during World War II. As they observe, 'Wartime censorship told the mass media what not to make known' and what should be included in films. 'Labor and capital buried their differences for a greater cause; class, ethnic and racial divisions evaporated in the foxholes and on the assembly line; even estranged family members were reconciled through the agency of war.'[123]

The OWI's Hollywood office, the Bureau of Motion Pictures, run by Lowell Mellett, aimed to promote the war effort and regulate the industry, studio films, screen content and cinematic messages that were permitted in wartime productions. It promoted six acceptable themes to convey in films:

1. Issues – Why we fight,
2. The Enemy – Whom we fight,
3. United Nations & Allied peoples,
4. Work & Production,
5. The Homefront,
6. The Fighting Forces.

As OWI chief Elmer Davis explained, 'The easiest way to inject a propaganda idea into most people's minds is to let it go through the medium of an entertainment picture when they do not realize that they are being propagandized'.[124] However, this new propaganda remit resulted in a complex regulatory labyrinth where various censorship agencies such as Washington's Office of War Information, its Bureau of Motion Pictures in Los Angeles, the government's Office of Censorship, Army and Navy branches of the US military, Hollywood studios and the film industry's self-regulation from the Production Code Administration had different, competing and contradictory censorship agendas.

The federal government's OWI Bureau of Motion Pictures regulated Hollywood industry motion pictures and cinematic screen content in 1942–1943. However, Washington's Office of Censorship sanctioned violent propaganda in films to aid the war effort, which directly conflicted with the industry's Production Code censorship that previously shunned screen violence and avoided political propaganda. Richard Jewell notes the 'slow process of PCA liberalization' throughout the war as the OWI Bureau of Motion Pictures discouraged 'any cinematic moment that might compromise the vision of an all powerful, utopian United States, from realistically gruesome battle scenes abroad to black market activity at home'.[125] The federal Office of Censorship banned cinematic depictions of gangsters in Hollywood films as 'un-American' screen material that could be used as Nazi propaganda and thus censored their illegal, unpatriotic incarnation in motion pictures during wartime.[126]

In a December 9, 1942 OWI letter to Hollywood executives, 'For the benefit of both your studio and the Office of War Information', Bureau of Motion Pictures director Lowell Mellett wrote, 'it would be advisable to establish a routine procedure whereby our Hollywood office would receive copies of studio treatments or synopses of all stories which you contemplate producing and of the finished scripts.'[127] He insisted that the government agency was not interested in censoring films and went on to explain:

This will enable us to make suggestions as to the war content of motion pictures at a stage when it is easy and inexpensive to make any changes which might be recommended. We should like also to set up as a routine procedure an arrangement whereby our Hollywood office might view all pictures in the long cut. While this is rather late in the operation to introduce any new matter it would make it possible for us to recommend the deletion of any material which might be harmful to the war effort.[128]

In May 1943, Mellett reiterated his position and added that it was merely a voluntary process:

Our reviewers in Hollywood read scripts when submitted and present to the producers immediately such views as result and offer such suggestions as may seem to be of value. There is a clear understanding on the part of the producers that they are completely free to disregard any of our views or suggestions; that we have no authority enabling us to force our views upon them and have never desired any such authority. In effect our operation is largely one of keeping producers informed of wartime problems and conscious of possible implications of proposed pictures or details of pictures.[129]

However, Hollywood filmmakers such as producer Walter Wanger protested that Mellett and the OWI

wanted all motion pictures shown to him in the rough, or long, version, before cutting. These requests caused apprehension within the industry. Outside, editors generally took the position that a threat to freedom of speech in one medium affected all. That conclusion is logical and sums the national mind. Censorship before utterance is abhorrent to Americans, who believe that autocracy can have no deadlier weapon than a blue pencil.[130]

Yet, ultimately, despite resistance from filmmakers like Wanger, by 1943, Hollywood film studios (with the exception of Paramount) regularly submitted scripts to the OWI.[131] In particular, the federal Office of War Information and Office of Censorship regulated motion picture images of the wartime homefront and combat front, as well as graphic newsreels of the conflict. Hollywood combat feature films, such as *Sahara* (1943) starring Humphrey Bogart, showed the US armed forces on battlefronts overseas (set in the African Sahara, shot in California and Arizona deserts) joining with multiethnic troops from Allied nations around the world to fight the enemy. Dramatic films such as *Mrs. Miniver* (1942), *Tender Comrade* (1943, with Ginger Rogers embodying the spirit of 'Rosie the Riveter' working on the assembly line) and *Since You Went Away* (1944) depicted women holding down the homefront in the US and the Allied nation of Great Britain doing their part to aid the war effort. Other films such as Fritz Lang's *Hangmen Also Die* (1943), an independent production released through non-MPPDA member studio United Artists, challenged Production Code censors in depicting Gestapo violence, torture, genocide and assassination in Nazi occupied Czechoslovakia and defied the Advertising Code with the bold tagline, 'Kill...Kill...Kill...Kill...'.

Combat documentaries such as *Memphis Belle* (1944) showed colour images of the war with gritty aerial footage of Allied bombing flights over Germany. Screen violence, which had been banned in newsreels, grew more graphic after the government's Office of Censorship allowed greater brutality in films for propaganda purposes, as seen in John Huston's combat documentary, *The Battle of San Pietro*, which was shot in 1944 and shown in 1945.[132] However, propaganda films made for and commissioned by the federal government were still subject to censorship in wartime. For example, John Ford was worried that his combat documentary, *The Battle of Midway*, which was shot on location with hand-held cameras as the battle started in the Pacific in 1942, would be censored; so he included footage of President Roosevelt's son and a marine which resulted in FDR proclaiming, 'I want every mother in America to see this film'. The short was distributed by Twentieth Century-Fox and won an Oscar for Best Documentary for 1942. Yet, colour combat footage of US casualties and burials at sea where servicemen hoisted military coffins to slide off the ship into the Pacific Ocean were cut from the film so as not to undermine a victorious propaganda piece.[133] By 1945, Frank Capra's propaganda film *Know the Enemy: Japan*, a racist depiction of the Japanese which arrived at the front (and was censored by General MacArthur) three days after the US dropped the atomic bomb on Hiroshima (with devastating, horrific results) and John Huston's *Let There Be Light*, about post-traumatic-stress disorder suffered by combat veterans in military hospitals, were seized and not shown to troops or the American public.[134] Other films produced in wartime, such as crime films, also faced censorship.

Censoring Wartime Crime Films

Hollywood produced an array of patriotic espionage crime and combat films to support the war effort, including *This Gun for Hire* (1942), *Casablanca* (1942), *Sahara, Hangmen Also Die, Passage to Marseille* (1944) and *To Have and Have Not* (1944). In 1941–1942, Paramount transformed Graham Greene's 1936 pre-war British espionage novel, *A Gun for Sale*, into patriotic crime movie, *This Gun for Hire*, a film noir set in 1940s wartime America where violent assassin Raven (Alan Ladd), aided by beautiful undercover FBI spy, Ellen (Veronica Lake), thwarts a Japanese bomb plot. After Breen left the PCA to run RKO, the PCA's Geoffrey Shurlock objected to the film's violence, illicit sex, nudity, homosexuality, disrespect toward the law, juvenile delinquency and 'inappropriate' language and behaviour, which violated the Code. Yet, much of the film's violence and sexual innuendo remained in the film. Although the PCA banned showing excessive graphic violence and sought to 'avoid gruesomeness' and 'details of committing crime', a gangster disguised as a servant (Marc Lawrence) describes macabre plans to commit and cover-up murder with great delight and murders were committed, including killing a cat, shooting saboteurs and gunning down a witness through a door.[135] Despite the fact that gangsters were censored during the war and that the film centered on an antiheroic killer assassin, *This Gun for Hire* was promoted as a patriotic gangster film about a 'Trigger Man' tapping into the wartime reception climate.[136]

Fortunately, Warner Bros.' war-torn romance *Casablanca*, about 'an American nightclub owner in Morocco who helps an anti-Nazi couple escape to America via Lisbon',[137] began filming a month before the OWI was created. However, Breen returned to the PCA in May 1942 and objected to several issues in *Casablanca*, including the film's portrayal of corrupt official Renault (Claude Rains) exploiting and sleeping with women who were desperate for exit visas and the adulterous 'suggestion' that Ilsa (Ingrid Bergman) was having an illicit sexual relationship with Rick (Humphrey Bogart) while she was married. On May 21, 1942, Breen insisted, 'Specifically, we cannot approve the present suggestion that Capt. Renault makes a practice of seducing the women to whom he grants visas. Any such inference of illicit sex could not be approved in the finished picture.' He added: 'The suggestion that Ilsa was married all the time she was having her love affair with Rick in Paris seems unacceptable and could not be approved in the finished picture. Hence, we request the deletion of Ilsa's line "Even when I knew you in Paris."'[138] Originally, in Murray Burnett and Joan Alison's *Everybody Comes to Rick's* (unproduced) play on which *Casablanca* is based, Bergman's character was a sophisticated unmarried 'single' woman called Lois who engaged in sexual affairs. Warners hoped casting a more virtuous Bergman in the role might help gain PCA approval. Since Breen was concerned that the script would not imply any illicit sex or that Ilsa slept with Rick when she comes to plead for letters of transit, director Michael Curtiz cut from the couple passionately embracing to a shot of them (still fully dressed) in conversation smoking cigarettes to imply sex rather than showing it.

Ernest Hemingway's *To Have and Have Not* was also changed from a pre-war 1937 story of unsavoury deeds set in Cuba to a wartime call for action and resistance to the Gestapo in French Martinique. Howard Hawks' film was seen as something of a follow up to *Casablanca*, starring Humphrey Bogart as a reluctant, unlikely patriot aiding the Free French. Writer William Faulkner moved the setting of *To Have and Have Not* to Martinique after the US Office of the Coordinator of Inter-American Affairs was opposed to harming Cuban-American relations with a wartime ally. Although the PCA cleaned up much of the censorable prostitution, illegal activity and ethnic slurs in Hemingway's novel, the film's suggestive hard-boiled dialogue remained, including abundant sexual innuendo and the salacious line by nineteen-year old newcomer Lauren 'The Look' Bacall, who famously says to Bogart, 'You know how to whistle, don't you, Steve? You just put your lips together and blow.'[139]

The Production Code was rapidly becoming antiquated in the wake of World War II, which 'unleashed forces that Hollywood could not ignore'. As Leonard Leff and Jerold Simmons observe: 'The 1930 proscriptions against violence and murder and especially adultery and illicit sex, now seemed outmoded; the endless stream of movies about fearless warriors and faithful wives old-fashioned.' In fact, 'Just beyond the door of the Production Code Administration on Hollywood Boulevard, sex was in the ozone'.[140]

Controversial, formerly-banned material like James M. Cain's hard-boiled 'red meat' pulp fiction, was adapted by Hollywood in wartime 'film noir' crime pictures, *Double Indemnity* (1944), *Mildred Pierce* (1945) and *The Postman Always Rings Twice* (1946), which challenged PCA censorship with scandalous topics. In the atmospheric chiaroscuro milieu of films noir *Double Indemnity, The Big Sleep* (1946) and *Gilda* (1946), censorship forced filmmakers to find interesting ways around the Code and encouraged cinematic artistry. In adapting Cain's story for noir *Double Indemnity*, about doomed insurance salesman, Walter Neff (Fred MacMurray) and dangerous married femme fatale, Phyllis (Barbara Stanwyck), who seduces him into an adulterous affair to murder her husband for cash, director/co-writer Billy Wilder and co-writer Raymond Chandler created an ominous setting of murder and deception.

Double Indemnity's shadowy 'black' visual style suggested censorable deeds. Salacious repartee in the film's dialogue amplified sexual innuendo yet technically complied with the Code. Dressed only in a towel when Neff arrives at her home, Phyllis has nothing on underneath. She descends the stairs buttoning her dress as he eyes her anklet and says he'd have to 'drive it around the block a couple of times' when he asks her name.

PHYLLIS: There's a speed limit in this state, Mr. Neff. Forty-five miles
  an hour.
NEFF: How fast was I going officer?
PHYLLIS: I'd say around ninety.
NEFF: Suppose you get down off your motorcycle and give me a ticket.
PHYLLIS: Suppose I let you off with a warning this time.

Phyllis coyly flirts with him, saying 'I wonder if I know what you mean.' He replies, 'I wonder if you wonder.' Such evocative verbal foreplay written for the film (not in Cain's novel) ran circles around the Code and implied deviant sexual intimacy. Yet, Neff's guilty 'voice of doom' narration expressed regret for his crimes and crime-fighting investigator Keyes (Edward G. Robinson) ensured justice and 'compensating moral values' prevailed. Wilder shot an alternate ending in which Walter is executed in a gas chamber for his crimes, but it was deemed too morbid. Instead, *Double Indemnity* ends with Walter killing and being shot by Phyllis, then confessing and collapsing after Keyes warns him 'You'll never even make the elevator' trying to escape and finally lays dying on the floor as Keyes calls the authorities.

Shot in late 1943, *Double Indemnity* was a censorship milestone opening the floodgates in Hollywood on filming the adulterous sex, violence and murder in Cain fiction—overturning the PCA ban of studios producing *Double Indemnity* in 1935 and *The Postman Always Rings Twice*

Phyllis (Barbara Stanwyck) greets Neff (Fred MacMurray) in a towel in *Double Indemnity*. (Paramount, 1944)

in 1934. Further, Wilder and Chandler cleverly subverted federal regulation by immediately stating that events in *Double Indemnity* occurred on July 16, 1938, before the war began, to make clear it does not depict a wartime setting and avoided interference by the OWI in censoring content for propaganda purposes.

While censors insisted there had been no easing of PCA censorship, such films noir, their censorable screen content, growing trend, and reception in contemporary 1940s film industry trade papers discourse reveal otherwise. In fact, by November 1944, the *New York Times* reported that Hollywood would 'depend' on '"red meat" stories of illicit romance and crime for a major share' of its productions.[141] Industry observer Fred Stanley opined that the 'Hollywood Crime and Romance' screen 'trend toward such material, previously shunned for fear of censorship, is traced by observers to Paramount's successful treatment of the James M. Cain novel, *Double Indemnity* which was described by some producers as "an emancipation for Hollywood writing"'.[142] Alfred Hitchcock proclaimed, 'Since *Double Indemnity*, the two most important words in motion pictures are Billy Wilder'. *Los Angeles Times* reported, 'Film History Made by *Double Indemnity*', regarding Code 'taboos' it 'overrides' detailing the 'actual commission of a crime' of 'passion... But it never tries to whitewash the criminals... like the great French cinemas, it is adult.'[143] *Hollywood Reporter* clamoured: 'With his *Double Indemnity* ... Billy Wilder has broken open a door hitherto locked to all those connected with the creation of motion pictures. He has made the hero and heroine of his stark drama a pair of murderers. There is no gloss to their wrong-doing, no sugar frosting to make palatable their misdeeds. It is a drama the like of which no other picture in recent memory brings to mind, more than a little reminiscent of the late lamented, excellent French technique.' It concluded that *Double Indemnity* 'will prove that Wilder has indeed broken down the door in which the taboos of this industry have been too long stored away.'[144] Hitchcock recognised the censorable noir underworld of illicit deeds. 'The setting is night. The corner of a street in the city. The ground... has cobbles washed with water by rain... under the street light... so we have the atmosphere for terror. Now, a person looks through a window. A black cat runs along the wall. And we wait for the limousine to come and go "da-da-da-da-da-da-da-da-da".'[145]

For *Phantom Lady* (1944, adapting a Cornell Woolrich story), PCA censors warned producer Joan Harrison and director Robert Siodmak about depicting excessive drinking, drug use, suggestive dancing and expressed concern jazz musicians were 'dope addicts' in a rowdy 'jive' music sequence in a jazz cellar with a sexual 'orgiastic' drum solo by Elisha Cook, Jr. The jam session included tight Cubistic framing and Dutch angles of shimmying legs and breast shots and a power angle of Ella Raines posing as a 'hep kitten' femme prostitute. The film included misogynistic violence where Raines is shoved, roughed-up and bruised by Cook in a fight, before he is killed by a mysterious serial-killer (Franchot Tone). In keeping with the wartime production context, Breen sent the script to Latin American advisor Addison Durland to consider 'Latin American angles of the story',[146] which included a dance performance by Carmen Miranda's sister, Brazilian star Aurora. Despite the Production Code or Advertising Code, publicity for *Phantom Lady* promoted the film noir's sexual violence and misogynism in beating the heroine onscreen and bruising the actress during rehearsals for filming.[147]

James M. Cain observed Hollywood producers 'have got hep to the fact that plenty of real crime takes place every day and that it makes a good movie... The public is fed up with the old-fashioned melodramatic type of hokum.'[148] Yet, in September 1944, the PCA rejected Paramount's first script for Billy Wilder's *The Lost Weekend* because censors considered its story of an alcoholic man who spends an entire weekend drunk to be unacceptable to the Code. Undeterred, Wilder began filming with an incomplete screenplay in October 1944 and Paramount sent sections of the script to PCA censors as it was finished. PCA censors also objected to the film's depiction of prostitution and its 'characterization of Gloria as a prostitute type' and insisted 'it will be absolutely essential to give her some legitimate occupation... Perhaps defining her as a buyer who entertains out of town visitors... would solve this problem.'[149] The film went on to win Oscars for Best Picture and Best Director.

However, in 1945, New York state (and cities Atlanta and Milwaukee in 1946) banned director Fritz Lang's film noir *Scarlet Street* (1945), an independent film produced by Lang and Walter Wanger's Diana Productions released through Universal, for its 'immorality' and excessive violence, which included a brutal ice pick murder of its duplicitous femme fatale Kitty (Joan Bennett). By January 1946, Wanger negotiated with New York censor Irwin Conroe, and *Scarlet Street* was approved after minor editorial cuts to reduce the number of ice pick stabs in the film's murder scene.[150]

Edward G. Robinson brutally stabs Joan Bennett with an ice pick in *Scarlet Street*. (Diana Productions, 1945)

Nonetheless, the femme fatale's dodgy boyfriend (Dan Duryea) is framed, jailed and executed for her murder, while the film's guilty betrayed anti-hero, Chris Cross (Edward G. Robinson), attempts suicide, goes crazy and hears their dead voices calling him in his head—but gets away with murder in the end.

All in all, *Scarlet Street* was quite censorable to the Code. Universal had to justify the film's lack of 'compensating moral values' in public to state and local censor boards since its anti-heroic noir protagonist is not punished or arrested for breaking the law and killing the deceitful femme fatale. The fact that Lang's noir film was released with a number of Code violations, despite its provocative content deemed so 'salacious' and unsavoury to the censors, anticipated future lapses in PCA screen censorship in years to come. After several decades, the Hays era was drawing to a close in 1945 at the MPPDA, soon to be rebranded the 'MPAA' under new leadership. Long known as the 'Hays Office', the PCA—and Breen's censorial leadership of the Hollywood film industry's self-regulation—would continue without Hays in the post-war era.

3   POST-WAR DEVELOPMENTS

Will Hays retired from the MPPDA at the end of World War II, amid an array of changes across the globe. After the death of President Roosevelt, the horror of the Holocaust, the graphic brutality of combat and the dropping of atomic bombs on Hiroshima and Nagasaki in Japan, it was a new beginning. Hays was replaced by former US Chamber of Commerce president Eric Johnston to head the MPPDA, which was renamed the Motion Picture Association of America (MPAA). As we will see, in the post-war era, Hollywood's self-regulation by the MPAA would face a litany of Code challenges and lapses in PCA censorship.

Post-war Industry Changes and Hollywood Film Censorship

Even more changes were ahead for the American film industry. Film historian Matthew Bernstein chronicles the extraordinary cinematic reception context for *Scarlet Street* and film noir amid the social and cultural tensions in the wake of World War II thus:

> Americans pondered the moral and practical ramifications of the nuclear age, the incredible revelations of Nazi war crimes and the communist menace whose dimensions were just emerging. On the home front, equally troubling issues had arisen: strikes for better wages were long past due and erupted around the country,

while returning veterans and women in the workforce complicated traditional notions of how the nuclear family functioned. And at the beginning of 1946, there was considerable controversy about the role movies had played in aggravating the social ills perceived in American society, particularly in relation to the family.[151]

As censorable film noir proliferated by the end of the war, the *New York Times* proclaimed that the 'high mark' of Hollywood's 'red meat' crime cycle—later renamed 'film noir'—was MGM's decision to produce hard-boiled writer James M. Cain's lusty murder story, *The Postman Always Rings Twice* (with stars John Garfield and Lana Turner), after ten years of collecting dust on the shelf, following the MPPDA banning studios from adapting the novel a decade earlier. Industry analyst Fred Stanley noted that the story was 'kept in the studio's archives until now because (to use a favored

Love at Laguna Beach: John Garfield and Lana Turner in *The Postman Always Rings Twice.* (MGM, 1946)

Hollywood expression) [of MGM's] inability to clean it up' for censors until the 'red meat' trend became popular with filmmakers and cinemagoers.[152] Cain's *The Postman Always Rings Twice* had been called 'strong men's meat and not for those who mind blood and raw lust. It has vigor and economy of method... but its artistic merit won't keep it from giving the sensitive nightmares.'[153] After the success of *Double Indemnity*, MGM decided to finally adapt *The Postman Always Rings Twice* as a film and Breen assured religious groups it would 'not be offensive'.[154]

At Breen's behest, MGM cleaned up the novel, shined bright light on the sets and made sure Lana Turner wore white to signify purity and please PCA censors, albeit as hamburgers sizzled on the grill to suggest sexual innuendo. Nonetheless, while the film featured adulterous lovers committing murder and a deadly femme fatale with skimpy hot pants and a halter top looking very sexy, the publicity suggested even more as *The Postman Always Rings Twice* was described as 'Love at Laguna Beach'— 'torrid' and 'too hot to handle' with 'savage boldness' as the couple kissed in swimsuits near the waves and taglines clamored: 'You must be

He had to have her love...If he hung for it! Garfield and Turner kiss in *The Postman Always Rings Twice*. (MGM, 1946)

a she-devil', 'Their Love was a Flame That Destroyed!' and 'He had to have her love... If he hung for it!', describing Cain's 'Sultry Novel of Love and Violence!' as 'SUITABLE ONLY FOR ADULTS', 'THE NOVEL THEY SAID WAS TOO DARING FOR HOLLYWOOD!'[155]

Reverend H. Parr Armstrong of the Oklahoma City Council of Churches and national religious organisations were mortified.[156] Yet, revealing the evolution of PCA censors a decade after banning the story, on September 19, 1945, Breen wrote to Dr. Samuel McCrea Cavert of the Federal Council of Churches of Christ in America:

> We believe the finished picture will not be offensive to anyone. It is a psychological study of two murderers who seek to cheat justice, but who fail in the attempt. I need not tell you that Metro, in its screen production, has made many drastic changes in the story as told in the novel. I am certain that, while the film story is 'strong meat', it will be an acceptable picture for adults.[157]

As *The Postman Always Rings Twice* was approved by Breen and PCA censors, Leff and Simmons observe, 'The [PCA] Seal on *The Postman* would close the parenthesis on an era of Code enforcement; it would tell Hollywood to purchase the most salacious books and anticipate Production Code certification'.[158]

Several factors contributed to this easing of Code censorship after the war, as, culturally and industrially, Hollywood, America and the world abroad converted from wartime to a post-war economy. For one thing, Will Hays, who was a supporter of Breen and the PCA and had banned censorable screen adaptations for years—as early as 'the formula' in the mid-1920s—was forced to resign as MPPDA president in September 1945 after studios 'questioned his ability to solve the post-war problems facing the industry'.[159]

By 1946, it was a fresh start for the newly rebranded MPAA. Industry conditions affecting screen censorship transformed by the end of the war due to a number of influential developments which eventually dealt a blow to the classical studio system and its self-regulation. Hollywood's self-censorship enforcement by the MPAA's PCA was undercut by the 1948 Paramount Decision antitrust regulation to dismantle the Hollywood studio system oligopoly. An important factor ultimately undermining the enforcement of Code censorship was the US federal government reopening the Paramount antitrust case against the film industry in February 1944,[160] which was briefly preempted for the duration of the war. Just a few years later, by 1948, the Paramount US Supreme Court Decision effectively dismantled the vertical integration model of the classic studio system in the post-war era, forcing major studios to sell off their theatres and exhibition chains.

The post-war media industry also changed as the federal government removed a freeze on research, development and manufacturing of television, a new and soon to be very popular leisure activity. Further, the film industry also faced stiff competition from re-opened international film markets, bitter labour disputes and unrest, the government's House Un-American Activities Committee (HUAC) 'Red Scare' investigations of Hollywood studios and industry blacklisting of creative talent, increasing independent and 'runaway' production of films outside Hollywood, skyrocketing production costs and diminishing revenues after the cinema

Bogart beats tough guys with his gun as 'The Look' Bacall smolders and *The Big Sleep* publicity promotes violence. (Warner Bros., 1946)

box-office peaked in 1946—after this, film-going audiences moved away from major 'first run' theatres in urban centers to the suburbs with television and other competing leisure activities benefitting as a result.

These developments also undermined and 'dis-integrated' the classical studio system and its previous censorial self-regulation by the MPPDA, now the MPAA. Significantly, as controversial adaptations by studios challenged Code regulation in the post-war era and became more 'acceptable' to the PCA, film censorship began to ease as new trends of provocative Hollywood films, such as formerly-banned film noir stories, flourished and became increasingly palatable and possible to produce. Films with 'salacious' screen content, such as *Double Indemnity*, *Scarlet Street*, *The Postman Always Rings Twice*, *The Big Sleep*, *Gilda* and, especially, *The Outlaw*, blatantly defied the Production Code and PCA censorship amid this changing Hollywood regulatory climate over a decade after the Code's conception.

For instance, when asked about the spicy innuendo and horse-racing sexual banter between Humphrey Bogart and Lauren Bacall in the 1946 film noir adaptation of Raymond Chandler's hard-boiled novel *The Big Sleep*, producer-director Howard Hawks replied: 'They [the censors] said they were gonna object to it and then they thought it over and decided they liked it so much that they were gonna let it go. What they objected to was stuff that was made with the intention of being lewd and they said I never did that, so they let me get away with murder.' He admitted, 'The end of the story was done by censors. They read the script and they didn't care for the end Chandler wrote. They said, "Howard, you can't get away with this." And I said, "OK, you write a scene for me." And they did and it was a lot more violent, it was everything I wanted. I said, "I'll hire you fellows as writers."' Hawks explained, 'They wrote the scene where Bogart sent a fellow out the door to get shot. That isn't exactly new, but it worked. They had vagaries about censorship. I was able to talk most of the censors out of it.' As Hawks described Martha Vickers' character, femme fatale Carmen, 'I wanted her to be a well-dressed little girl who just happened to be a nymphomaniac'.[161] Hawks also bought the rights to Ernest Hemingway's novel *The Sun Also Rises*, 'about a fellow who was impotent', but never made the film. 'Censors wouldn't allow you to do the thing at the time. I did my best to try to figure out a way, but I never could figure it out' (Hawks later sold it to Darryl Zanuck at Twentieth Century-Fox).[162]

In the immediate aftermath of the war, by 1946 into 1947, American film censorship itself was gradually beginning to allow greater tolerance of social issues—as social problem films such as Billy Wilder's *The Lost Weekend* and William Wyler's *The Best Years of Our Lives* (1946) won critical acclaim and Academy Awards for Best Picture. Surprisingly, even screen censorship organisations such as the Production Code Administration penned public editorials to that effect and the Legion of Decency adopted new categories to accommodate 'tasteful', 'adult', 'mature' themes beyond 'general', 'family' viewing (targeting specific audience demographics suitable for adults, rather than children.) Such censorial transformation and changing cinematic reception conditions resonated in this post-war censorship and viewing climate amid a growing number of independent and art cinema productions. Many filmgoers and filmmakers had witnessed and experienced harsh realities—even combat—in real life overseas and seen the gritty, unvarnished 'newsreel style' and 'realism' of documentaries and

Edward G. Robinson watches *The Stranger* Orson Welles ensnare Loretta Young. (International Pictures, 1946)

'neorealism' of international films which challenged the strictures of the Code and became very popular in the wake of the conflict.[163]

By November 1947, the PCA's Geoffrey Shurlock, Breen's longtime assistant, acknowledged that suggestions from outside and within the film industry had called for the Production Code to be 'revised' and updated to 'meet new conditions'. Shurlock predicted that in the future the Code may possibly be 'amended' to accommodate 'more mature treatment' for a 'limited audience' of 'high quality entertainment for adults only'.[164]

Trailblazer Orson Welles called for 'adult' movie fare as early as 1945, telling the New York Times, 'I think [motion] pictures are in a bad way. They need revitalizing... for private film experimentation and a chain of adult theatres free from Hays office code censorship.' As Welles incorporated actual graphic documentary footage of the Nazi Holocaust genocide in his 1946 Gothic-espionage film noir The Stranger, he observed: 'Films dealing with serious and important subjects should be produced, even if the big boys have to be taxed for them.' Yet, after being denied producer credit (or any screen acknowledgement for his extensive behind-the-scenes creative contributions) for 1944's Jane Eyre (which merely lists him as the film's star), Welles ironically admitted, 'I do not like being an actor and I don't acknowledge the existence of a job called producer. The only thing I like in films is directing.'[165] Welles was not only denied screen credit (although he extensively contributed to the film's design, producing, directing, writing and performances), but was basically 'censored' and blackballed from making Hollywood films for a decade during the post-war era. After directing noir films The Stranger and The Lady From Shanghai (shot in late-1946 to early-1947 but not released until May 1948), Welles and other filmmakers made films 'in exile' in Europe as the 'Cold War' period took hold.

Yet even the National Catholic Legion of Decency was distinguishing between different levels of films aimed at 'general' versus 'adult' viewing audiences after the war. In 1947, Hollywood trade journal Motion Picture Herald published the Legion of Decency ratings of films, which included 'adult' as well as 'general' ratings of pictures in a variety of categories. For example, RKO's The Farmer's Daughter (1947), MGM's It Happened in Brooklyn (1947) and Paramount's The Perils of Pauline (1947) were rated A-1–'unobjectionable'–and classified as suitable for 'general' audiences. United Artists' independent jazz musical New Orleans (1947) starring Louis Armstrong and Billie Holliday was classified as 'general' but was rated A-2 'unobjectionable for adults.' However, there was a distinction between these 'general' (family) viewing films and films noir, such as Columbia's Humphrey Bogart picture *Dead Reckoning* (1947), MGM's Raymond Chandler adaptation *Lady in the Lake* (1946) and Warner Bros.' *Pursued* (1947), which were considered and classified as 'adult' and rated A-2 'unobjectionable for adults.' The Legion had likewise given Billy Wilder's iconic film noir *Double Indemnity* an A-2 rating for its eroticization of murder and rated *The Postman Always Rings Twice* as B 'objectionable in part' for its sympathetic portrayal of murderous lovers. While Twentieth Century-Fox's *The Ghost and Mrs. Muir* (1947) and *Miracle on 34th Street* (1947) were classified as suitable for 'general' audiences, both films were rated B 'objectionable in part' by the Legion. RKO's Jean Renoir Gothic-noir thriller *The Woman on the Beach* (1947)—starring Joan Bennett, Robert Ryan and Charles Bickford in a haunting, mysterious 'love triangle'—was considered and classified as 'adult' and rated B 'objectionable in part' by the Legion.[166]

In a changing American landscape of evolving gender roles, Hollywood films faced a gender-bias in these censorial organisations and their representational constraints. Most US film censors were men, typically religious (white Catholic heterosexual) men, regulating cinema to specify and decide how women, sexuality and people of colour were portrayed onscreen. The Legion of Decency emphasised this gendered landscape specifically referring to its all-male censorial board in its publications: *Motion pictures classified by National Legion of Decency: a moral estimate of entertainment feature motion pictures / prepared under the direction of the National Office of the Legion of Decency with the co-operation of the Motion Picture Department of the International Federation of Catholic Alumnae, and a male board of consultors* [emphasis added].[167] Their all-male censors certainly projected their ideas of decency and sexuality (or lack thereof) on films. Although the 1947 *Motion Picture Herald* journal did not list films as 'Condemned' by the Legion of Decency, the censorial battles over Howard Hughes' Western *The Outlaw* were another matter altogether.

Defying Censors: The Return of The Outlaw

After withdrawing *The Outlaw* from distribution following a one-week 1943 run during the war, Hughes redoubled his challenge to the censors when he re-released his controversial film in 1946 with unapproved advertising.

Publicity for *The Outlaw* featured sensational taglines with tabloid images of a scantily-clad sex siren Jane Russell that emphasised her cleavage to titillate (male) moviegoers. However, even other film industry executives balked at the outrageous, censorable images. Twentieth Century-Fox production chief Darryl Zanuck penned a letter to 'My dear Joe' Breen on April 2, 1946, writing: 'You know I do not want to make trouble for you. You have a very difficult job and I believe I appreciate it more than most producers. However, when an ad like [*The Outlaw*] appears in the paper after the conference we had the other day, I have a hell of a job keeping my boys in line. The whole campaign on this picture is a disgrace to the industry and I am on the verge of publicly attacking Howard Hughes with a blast in the newspapers. Before I do so I would like your opinion as I do not want to do anything that would adversely affect you or your organization. I am also furious with [independent producer Walter] Wanger. I believe he has deliberately capitalized on the censorship trouble with *Scarlet Street* and while I don't blame him at all for making money, I think it is bad money and that in the final run he will have to pay for it: however, my main fury is at the *The Outlaw* advertisements. The major [studio] companies make many mistakes but I have never seen any major company resort to such cheap vulgarity as this.'[168]

Not surprisingly, the MPAA industry trade association's New York office condemned *The Outlaw*'s 'unapproved', 'salacious' exploitation and advertising. In an April 9, 1946 letter to Hughes, the MPAA insisted the film's unapproved advertising was 'grounds' for Hughes' 'suspension or expulsion from membership' in the MPAA for violating by-laws which required that filmmakers must honour 'standards of fair representation and good taste in the advertising of motion pictures' and must submit all advertising in advance to be approved by the Advertising Code Administration.[169] This censorial dustup over *The Outlaw* was quite remarkable given that the industry Advertising Code was more lenient than the Production Code.

Nevertheless, Hughes persevered with his sex Western. When *The Outlaw* was screened in San Francisco a few weeks later, police arrested the theatre manager for showing a picture 'offensive to decency' and seized prints of the film. (He was later released.) Hughes then resigned from and sued the MPAA for 'violating the First Amendment of the Constitution of the United States' and antitrust laws, in its system of film industry regulation enforced by monetary penalties on filmmakers if a film was denied a seal of

The Picture That Couldn't Be Stopped! Jane Russell's scandalous publicity for *The Outlaw*. (Hughes Productions, 1943)

approval and using coercive tactics to force members to comply with MPAA demands. The MPAA countersued that they had not breached their legal contract and Breen revoked the Production Code seal from *The Outlaw* for not submitting 'all advertising and publicity material' for approval, insisting that Hughes remove the PCA 'seal of approval' from all prints of *The Outlaw* since it did not comply with the Advertising Code.

In the midst of these legal battles, Hughes capitalised on and exploited the censorship controversy. He promoted the uproar and independent distributor United Artists (UA) 'roadshowed' *The Outlaw* in theatres, touring the United States in 1946–1947 with a grand publicity campaign that included flying skywriters and an aerial blimp. Billboards and posters for *The Outlaw* carried sensational headlines about Hughes' 'forbidden', censored sex Western as 'THE PICTURE THAT COULDN'T BE STOPPED!'. Yet the film continued to encounter censorship bans and drew protests across America. Catholic Archbishop John Cantwell was mortified by *The Outlaw* and asserted in *The Tidings* Catholic newspaper that no Catholic could see the film 'with a free conscience'.[170]

As luck would have it, in May 1946 Minneapolis theaters replaced *The Outlaw* with *The Postman Always Rings Twice*, notorious for its decade-long censorship challenges. After receiving complaints from religious leaders, the Interstate Circuit in Texas refused to show *The Outlaw*. By September

1946, municipal Judge E. Paul Mason banned the film's exhibition in Maryland because Russell's 'breasts hung like a thunderstorm over a summer landscape'. State censors protested to the PCA that Hughes' lawyers tried to force the Kansas censor board to approve *The Outlaw* without any cuts. When Hughes refused to cut the film, Ohio State censors banned *The Outlaw* in December 1946. *Hollywood Reporter* claimed theatre projectionists engaged in 'inadvertent' censorship of *The Outlaw* by clipping out 'hot' scenes for their private collections. But the mayor of Indianapolis, Indiana insisted *The Outlaw* was 'just a western' and refused to ban it.[171]

Overseas, the British press panned *The Outlaw* after an uncensored version screened in London in November 1946, but praised Hughes for battling the MPAA. In the provinces, the *Sunderland Echo* declared, 'This long-delayed attack on American censorship is welcome, for if Hughes wins his case it will open the way to more wholehearted sincerity in American films and will provide a better market for British films'. However, the film's advertising drew ire as a huge banner of Russell received a 'nudity complaint' from the London County Council.[172]

Back in the States, by November 1946 the National Board of Review of Motion Pictures publicly criticised the New York censor board for banning *The Outlaw*. In December 1946, when New York City's licensing commissioner tried to have the film's license revoked, the New York State Board of Regents found they did not have authority to do so. In January 1947, they requested the New York state legislature give the Department of Education

The Outlaw publicity blimp: Kept Off The Screen For Three Years – It's Coming At Last! (Hughes Productions, 1943)

authority to revoke film licenses on the basis of suggestive advertising. In US Congressional hearings in November 1947 on Hughes' World War II military contracts, General Bennett Meyers stated that Hughes authorised him to pay $150,000 to the Legion of Decency, which had 'Condemned' the picture, to try to reverse the New York ban. (Hughes denied Meyers' claim, insisting it was not worth buying off the Legion.) The New York licensing commissioner lifted the ban on *The Outlaw* a year later in September 1947 after objectionable material was sufficiently changed. When *The Outlaw* opened in New York on September 11, 1947, with 'cleaned-up' advertising, it was shown around-the-clock, 24-hours-a-day.[173]

In spite of—or rather because of—the film's controversy with Hollywood industry and state/local censors, *The Outlaw* ultimately broke box-office records. By February 1947, *Hollywood Reporter* suggested the film must have been seen by about 65 per cent of the population in cities where it was shown. In August 1948, after Hughes became RKO studio production chief, RKO bought the rights to release *The Outlaw* (from UA), but was unable to distribute it because the film lacked a PCA Code seal. But in October 1949, in response to editorial revisions by Hughes, the PCA restored *The Outlaw*'s seal and the Legion of Decency reversed its 'Condemned' 'C' rating. The film, which cost $1,200,000, had already made $4,500,000 and grossed a further $2,600,000 for RKO by April 1952. As censorship eased in the 1950s-1960s, *Hollywood Reporter* noted *The Outlaw* had made over $20 million by 1968.[174]

Crossfire *and* Act of Violence: *Social Realism, Censorship and the Blacklist*

When considering post-war Hollywood censorship, the question remains: did the blacklist in Hollywood represent a form of actual or intended censorship or 'propaganda'? Amid a growing 'Red Scare' climate with the US government's House Un-American Activities Committee (HUAC) hearings and investigations of Hollywood by October 1947, provocative, controversial screen material was certainly avoided as new MPAA president Eric Johnston frowned on disreputable, downbeat noir crime pictures and vowed, 'We'll have no more films that show the seamy side of American life'.[175] Johnston discouraged progressive social realism, liberal causes and topical issues as in post-war social problem films, insisting 'We'll have no more *Grapes of Wrath*, we'll have no more *Tobacco Roads*'.[176]

Critically acclaimed social problem films such as *Crossfire* (1947) championed hard-hitting social realism in raising serious issues, which were not targeting an audience of younger children, but rather aimed at more mature viewers. Not insignificantly, *Crossfire* dealt with the pervasive exposure to brutal violence as a result of military combat and the global conflict's potential to foster hate and xenophobia, such as anti-Semitism in the wake of the genocide of the Holocaust. The powerful film tackled hate, ethnic prejudice, intolerance and anti-Semitism and faced censorship of its original theme of homosexuality concerning a gay hate crime murder by a veteran.

Two years earlier, in 1945, PCA censor Joseph Breen insisted that the script of *Crossfire* violated the Hollywood Production Code. Based on Richard Brooks' hard-hitting 1945 novel *The Brick Foxhole*, about a veteran who kills a homosexual, the film's working title was that of the book and, later, *Cradle of Fear*. Initially, Breen and PCA censors took issue with the homophobic veteran antagonist Montgomery in Brooks' book who kills another man Samuels in a hate crime. The Production Code had banned homosexuality in films, as well as excessive violence and brutality. In a July 17, 1945 PCA letter to RKO executive William Gordon, censor Breen objected to the studio adapting the novel which he considered to be 'thoroughly and completely unacceptable, on a dozen or more counts'.[177]

Robert Ryan's bigoted hate leads him to murder Sam Levene in *Crossfire*. (RKO, 1947)

However, in the post-war climate of shock as the facts surrounding the Holocaust began to emerge, screenwriter John Paxton changed the homosexual hate crime in the story to that of an anti-Semitic murder of Samuels (now a Jew) and Breen approved the project, adding a cautionary warning that the eventual adaptation should not suggest homosexuality and should include 'no suggestion of a "pansy" characterization about Samuels or his relationship with the soldiers'.[178] On release, Crossfire was applauded for depicting anti-Semitism in the US. The New York Times called Crossfire one of Hollywood's first 1940s films to 'face questions of racial and religious prejudice with more forthright courage than audiences have been accustomed to expect'.[179]

Shot in 34 days on a lean $589,000 budget, Crossfire was a huge critical and box-office success, a 'sleeper' film grossing $1,270,000 that became the biggest hit for RKO in 1947. Crossfire was nominated for several Academy Awards, including Best Picture (losing to Twentieth Century-Fox's equally topical Gentleman's Agreement), Best Director, Best Screenplay (Adaptation), Best Supporting Actor (Robert Ryan) and Best Supporting Actress (Gloria Grahame) and won Best Social Film at the Cannes Film Festival in September 1947. By December 1947, the African-American magazine, Ebony, recognised Crossfire with an award for its tackling of social issues as a film 'improving interracial understanding'.[180]

However, the American film industry's post-war embrace of topical progressive social issues faced a virulent backlash in a growing Cold War climate of the 'Red Scare' and Hollywood blacklist which effectively purged liberal filmmakers and censored many productions, betraying many talented moviemaking careers in the process. In fact, Crossfire was the last RKO film for director Edward Dmytryk and producer Scott after Hughes took over the studio in May 1948. Even earlier, by October 1947, the US House Committee on Un-American Activities (HUAC) Congressional hearings had labelled a number of filmmakers, including Dmytryk and Scott, 'unfriendly' witnesses. Originally created by Congress in 1938 to investigate political extremists, in the post-war era, HUAC focused on exposing 'Communist', 'left-wing' activities in America and Hollywood after World War II. By late 1947, HUAC specifically targeted the film industry: 'Studios Strart Purging Staffs,' wrote the Hollywood Reporter.

Dmytryk and Scott were the first two members of the infamous 'Holly-wood Ten', producers, writers and directors indicted for contempt of

Congress after refusing to state whether they were or had been Communists. Other members of the Hollywood Ten were screenwriters Dalton Trumbo, John Howard Lawson, Ring Lardner, Jr., Albert Maltz, Samuel Ornitz, Alvah Bessie, Lester Cole and producer-director Herbert Biberman. By December 3, 1947, Hollywood studio executives signed the Waldorf Statement vowing to 'blacklist' 'Communists' and 'subversives' from working in the film industry and, in effect, instituting a 'Red Scare' purging liberal creative talent from Hollywood. In April 1948, the 'Hollywood Ten' were convicted of 'contempt of Congress' in Federal Court in Washington, DC. All ten filmmakers served prison terms and for many years were 'blacklisted' and banned from working in the Hollywood film industry, essentially censoring their work. (Several blacklisted writers continued to write under pseudonyms, which was more difficult for directors and producers to do.)

In January 1948, Dmytryk, who was just considered for a Best Director Oscar for *Crossfire*, lost his RKO contract after being indicted and then sued the studio for $1,783,425, claiming anguish, personal humiliation and loss of salary, screen fame and artistic reputation because of his firing. However, after imprisonment, by September 1950, Dmytryk was released from jail after testifying before HUAC in 1951 and admitting that he and Scott had been Communists. Filmmakers such as Dmytryk were forced to 'name names' and implicate others to be removed from Hollywood's blacklist. Dmytryk's next Hollywood film was the low-budget *Mutiny* (1952), but Scott remained blacklisted and never produced another film.

Like *Crossfire,* other social realist noir films, such as Fred Zinnemann's *Act of Violence* (produced in 1948, released in 1949), also dealt with hard-hitting topics and captured the fractious climate of this tumultuous, changing post-war era. In the wake of *Crossfire,* it is remarkable that *Act of Violence* was even produced in this strife ridden period. In fact, it was almost not produced. Intended as a Warner Bros. production, thematically, *Act of Violence* (originally titled 'The Traitor') deals with informing, disloyalty, subversion and what returning combat veterans did in the war to enable the burgeoning Cold War 'Red Scare' paranoia of the late-1940s. Early on, Warner Bros., director Don Siegel and producer Jerry Wald praised *Act of Violence* as a socially relevant film noir project like *Crossfire* and at one point Raoul Walsh was assigned to direct it. *Crossfire*'s Robert Mitchum, *High Sierra*'s noir icon Humphrey Bogart and *Laura/Best Years of Our Lives* star Dana Andrews were considered for the lead role.

In October 1947, as the HUAC hearings ramped up, Warner Bros. executives unexpectedly recommended eliminating night exterior scenes, which would have undercut and mitigated against *Act of Violence*'s dark, atmospheric noir style. Then, by December, Warner Bros. abruptly dropped the project and sold it to independent *Naked City* producer Mark Hellinger, who suddenly died a few weeks later. After several months with the project in limbo, MGM eventually acquired it in 1948.

Socially-minded executive Dore Schary had backed topical noir *Crossfire* at RKO before moving to MGM and supervising production on *Act of Violence*. When asked if he felt constrained by Production Code censorship, Schary insisted, 'I didn't worry at all. When I did worry, I challenged them. And I usually won. I see no objection to saying, "shit", I see no objection to saying, "damn", or "hell." And when I wrote a scene for *Battleground* [1949] and used the word, "bastard", I said to the Code office, "I'm going to put it in. Try and stop me."'[181] In terms of pressure from financial investors, Schary added: 'New York money wouldn't mind if you could get away with something a little daring... But if some banker had come in to see [MGM mogul Louis B.] Mayer and said, "Look, Louis, we want you to change the ending of this picture," Mayer would have screamed, "Get out of my office, or I'll punch you in the mouth. This is my studio and I'm making the picture."'[182]

Schary had left RKO after conservative Hughes took over the studio and immediately fired liberal filmmakers. Hughes had laid off three quarters of the RKO studio workforce in 1948 and production was virtually halted for six months. Hughes was also the first major studio executive to comply with signing the Paramount Decision Consent Decree to break up the classical Hollywood studio system and in doing so effectively undermine its system of industry self-censorship. As a result, paradoxically, Hughes shifted from functioning as a renegade independent filmmaker defying the American motion picture industry's PCA censorship of his films to eventually taking control of a major studio eliminating most of the creative talent from the Hollywood studio and, in the process, helping to break up the studio system itself. These post-war developments also exemplified how censorial restrictions on US films were shifting from an increasingly obsolete list of specific Production Code taboos on sex and screen violence to a new form of ideological constraints. The Cold War cultural climate of anti-Communist xenophobia was heightened in the McCarthy era of the 1950s. By 1951, HUAC renewed government hearings scrutinizing the American film industry, prompting the studios to institute an infamous 'blacklist' against liberal creative talent in Hollywood who were suspected of being Communists, sympathisers or 'fellow travelers', thus censoring their work and films.[183] Remembering the strife-ridden constrictions and cultural tensions of this post-war period, *Singin' in the Rain* director Stanley Donen recalled, 'How do you tell a story which has a human feeling? Because you don't dare have too many human feelings, they'll be thought of as "Communistic".'[184]

Indicative of the period's xenophobia and ideological constraints, MGM mogul Louis B. Mayer disparaged European émigré writer-director Billy Wilder, who filmed *Double Indemnity* and *The Lost Weekend,* as a 'foreigner' at Wilder's industry premiere for *Sunset Boulevard* (1950). In fact, in terms of the impact of Hollywood's Red Scare to potentially censor certain types of films from being made, memos from post-war studio executives suggest that by 1950, hard-hitting social realist and downbeat noir films were considered risky, dangerous and controversial in the industry, often drastically watered down by studio executives or not produced at all and basically avoided. For example, in a 1950 memo to Elia Kazan and John Steinbeck regarding *Viva Zapata!*, Twentieth Century-Fox production chief Darryl Zanuck stated it was important to be cautious and make 'very clear' a film 'isn't Communism... because, frankly, in the present script there is inadvertently a peculiar air about certain speeches, which might be interpreted by the Communists to claim that we are subtly working for them... we will all get kicked below the belt if it does not turn out to be a commercial as well as an artistic success. *Sunset Boulevard* was a masterpiece until it was released throughout the country and failed to do business. It is not so big a masterpiece today.'[185]

Further, Zanuck sent a 'CONFIDENTIAL' studio memo to 'All Producers and Directors' in 1950. 'We have completed our third survey of audience and box-office reaction to all pictures released during the last quarter. It is always difficult to speak in broad or general terms about the *reasons* for the success or failure of individual pictures—or even of groups of pictures—because there are always certain exceptions ... One thing stands out very clearly and that is the fact that the theatre-going public has been saturated with pictures of violence and films with underworld or "low" backgrounds.'[186]

In a confidential memo to director Henry King, Zanuck insisted there was little interest in censorable, social realist or noir crime films:

Audiences today, particularly in America, do not want pictures of violence or extreme brutality. In spite of the high quality of such pictures as *Panic in the Streets*, *Asphalt Jungle*, [Otto Preminger's 1950 noir] *Where the Sidewalk Ends*, etc., etc., these films and all films in this category have proved to be a shocking disappointment [...] Particularly, if they are 'downbeat' in nature or deal with sordid backgrounds, unsympathetic characters and over-emphasized 'suffering' [...] An exceptional picture of this nature manages to squeeze by occasionally. *The Men* is a disappointment and... disease in *Panic in the Streets* is one of the elements that contributed to the poor returns on this fine picture, which received unanimous praise from the critics.[187]

Zanuck argued, 'Pictures dealing with psychopathic characters have also outlived their usefulness *at this time*. There have been twenty-three pictures released in eighteen months in which one or more characters are motivated by psychopathic or psychiatric disorders. It has gotten so that this has become the standard motivation for practically all evildoers.' He concluded: 'Of course, again, there is always an exceptional picture that for other reasons may be able to survive at the box-office in spite of this handicap. But you cannot with any sense of security depend on this. Pictures in this category are certainly a very high risk.'[188] Thus, 'downbeat' films were avoided.

Hollywood's blacklist and the Red Scare affected many social realist and noir crime film writers, directors and creative talent who were politically liberal intellectuals affiliated with progressive causes, social politics, Depression-era populism, the anti-fascist Popular Front in World War II and even the Communist party—and who would be labelled 'Red' and a post-war threat in a conservative and xenophobic Cold War political climate. The influence of Italian neorealism was also significant in Hollywood's progressive push toward realistic 'message' pictures. Liberal socially-conscious creative talent coincided with other humanist and pacifist Marxist writers and neorealist directors in Italy opposing wartime fascism. Despite the ideological constraints of the era, after the global conflict of World War II, the post-war influx and popularity of socially-minded international cinema from re-opened overseas film markets challenged and ultimately undermined Hollywood censorship in myriad ways.

Post-war Censorship Challenges and Decline of the Code

An array of cultural changes and economic developments affected the film industry and contributed to a decline and easing of Hollywood's Production Code censorship from the late-1940s-1950s. Growing out of graphic images in World War II combat newsreels and the Korean War in 1950–53, there was a proliferation of images of violence and brutality which led to a desensitisation to and curiosity about graphic images onscreen, as in noir crime films and war-related documentaries. The publication of the *Kinsey Reports* on sexual behaviour regarding male sexuality in 1948 and female sexuality in 1953 and publication of *Playboy* magazine with its debut issue featuring a cover image and centerfold of a nude Hollywood film star Marilyn Monroe in 1953, contributed to a greater latitude, awareness and curiosity about sexuality in post-war American culture.

These post-war cultural and social developments made Hollywood's 1930 Production Code and its rigid censorial strictures seem antiquated and out-of-touch, both in the US and overseas, as was evident by the content of international films of this period. UNESCO's first International Conference of Artists in Venice, Italy in 1952 and the American Civil Liberties Union (ACLU) called for freedom from film censorship. In 1951 there were amendments to the Code and by 1955 there were calls to eliminate the PCA. In 1956, as a means for Hollywood to resist various pressure groups, a rating board (made up of parents, psychologists and social scientists) was suggested and the Code was revised.

By 1948, as the classical Hollywood studio system unraveled in the wake of antitrust enforcement, it is significant that the Paramount Decision also undermined the industry's self-regulation by the PCA. In fact, the antitrust ruling energised independent productions, which no longer worried about the Code Seal of Approval because they were not under the studio system's vertical integration of studio-owned theatres. In the wake of the 1948 antitrust decision, independent producers now had more places to show films and theatre venues were open to independents because the major studios no longer controlled exhibition. This post-war exhibition climate was different than the situation that existed during the war in 1942, when independent exhibitors or theatres affiliated with major studios could technically show films released without an official PCA Seal of Approval (in theory), but did not (in practice), because then they would not get the big budget major 'A' pictures to screen in their theatres. Further, aesthetically, cinematically and in terms of censorial constraints (or lack thereof), many post-war independent productions championed individual expression and included more provocative, frank content onscreen in treating film as a communication medium of ideas beyond entertainment. Increasingly, in the post-war era, filmmakers in Hollywood were against the specificities of the Code, although many agreed with its general moral principles.

Hollywood also had to respond to the popularity of television in the post-war era, which affected cinematic censorial constraints. As television became the increasingly pervasive mass medium in American homes after the war, Hollywood films strived to include what could not be shown on television and thus pushed for greater latitude in motion picture content. Ironically, then, television was an unexpected liberating factor for filmic screen content during this time. As television rose in popularity, more explicit screen content, which was censored on early TV, was embraced by Hollywood. Filmmakers endeavoured to draw audiences away from television screens and compete with foreign cinema by producing 'edgier' film adaptations of sensational or controversial novels and plays about 'taboo' subjects involving sex, violence, profanity and vulgarity with topical, provocative screen realism from the original source material. Hollywood film adaptations *Pitfall* (1948), *Forever Amber, Gentleman's Agreement, Flamingo Road* (1949), *Pinky* (1949), *The Asphalt Jungle* (1950), *Detective Story* (1951), *A Streetcar Named Desire* (1951) and *From Here to Eternity* (1953) defied the strictures of PCA screen censorship. In 1948 film noir *Pitfall*, 'we did have problems with the ending before the Hays Code would approve', director Andre de Toth admitted. 'You couldn't commit adultery. You couldn't say dirty words. For me this was always ridiculous... I want to photograph life. Film noir, Westerns, whatever kind of picture, I wanted real life.' (He received a code seal after subtly reminding censors about their own affairs.)[189]

In Otto Preminger's 1947 film adapting Kathleen Winsor's salacious, adulterous romance novel *Forever Amber*, Joseph Breen banned the story, about a tenacious woman who sleeps her way to the top in Restoration England, as 'utterly and completely unacceptable under any one of a dozen provisions of the Production Code' (Winsor's publisher promoted the ban). Twentieth Century-Fox public relations director (and former PCA executive), Colonel Jason Joy stated Fox was acquiring the screen rights after PCA officer

Geoffrey Shurlock agreed that censorial problems could be fixed. However, the Breen Office insisted 'the finished picture is objectionable because it deals excessively in illicit sex and adultery... in violation of the provisions of the Code' and the film was 50–60 per cent different from the script sent to the PCA. After censors suggested changes, Joy submitted two reels of re-edited and re-dubbed sequences and the film was approved. Breen also sent a three-page memo to MPPA president Eric Johnston in New York explaining his reasons for giving *Forever Amber* a Code seal.

Forever Amber broke opening day box-office records, but was condemned by the Legion of Decency. Cardinal Francis Spellman, Archbishop of New York, called it 'a glorification of immorality and licentiousness' and insisted 'Catholics may not see this production with a safe conscience'. Catholic Churches in Boston, Cincinnati, Providence and Indianapolis condemned the film and tried to legally stop screenings and the Archbishop of Philadelphia threatened to boycott Fox Theater if *Forever Amber* was not pulled within 48 hours. To reverse the Legion's 'C' rating, Fox added voice-over prologue and epilogue condemnations of sin, which Preminger was 'vehemently opposed' to and the Legion reclassified *Forever Amber* from a 'C' (condemned) to a 'B' (morally objectional in part) rating.[190] 'The Legion of Decency really emasculated the picture,' Preminger admitted.

There was an incredible scene in [Twentieth Century-Fox President] Spyros Skouras' office. The head of the Legion of Decency didn't even want to see the picture. He said to Skouras: 'We banned the book. Why did you buy it and make a picture?' And Skouras literally went down on his knees and said, 'Father, please, we invested 6 million dollars in this picture. Please. Go and look at it with Mr. Preminger.'

Preminger recalled that The Legion insisted on censorial changes for the picture and wanted the studio to change the title of *Forever Amber* because 'they felt it was very irreverent of Twentieth Century-Fox to make a film of a book that was banned. Finally, we had to put on a foreword that spoke about sin and how it is punished ("The wages of sin is death.") Then, whenever two people kissed, we had to dissolve or cut as their lips approached. Anyway, I don't think the film was a masterpiece one way or the other.'[191]

Topical post-war films like Elia Kazan's *Gentleman's Agreement* tackled anti-Semitism and *Pinky* dealt with racism and the oppression of minorities

Forever Amber was called 'a
glorification of immorality
and licentiousness.'
(Twentieth Century-Fox, 1947)

'passing' as white and an 'interracial' marriage in the segregated American South. However, *Pinky* cast a white actor as a light-skinned black because the PCA banned interracial 'miscegenation' sexual relationships onscreen. The NAACP called the original *Ladies' Home Journal* story (initially titled, *Quality*) 'the first time in any popular national magazine a short novel in which the protagonist was a Negro...dealt with apparent sympathy and realism with Negro problems in white society,' although upholding the status quo.[192] But the PCA worried about distribution/exhibition problems in the South, was concerned the industry would be accused of supporting President Truman's civil rights program, that new local/state censor boards would be established, and its release would spur Ku Klux Klan activity. Thus, Breen cautioned filmmakers to 'avoid physical contact between Negroes and whites, throughout this picture.'[193] (NAACP suggested scrapping the picture, but Darryl Zanuck defended it as conveying 'emotionally' the 'injustice and daily hurts suffered' by people of colour.)[194]

MGM 'whitewashed' objectionable Code 'miscegenation' in *Show Boat* (1950), casting Ava Gardner instead of Lena Horne as a light-skinned mulatto (even playing a recording of Horne's voice during Gardner's screen test).[195] Called 'the nation's top Negro entertainer,' Horne faced racism in Hollywood. She played the *Show Boat* role in MGM's *Till the Clouds Roll By*. Aljean Harmetz of the *New York Times* notes Horne was 'the first black performer to be signed to a long-term contract by a major Hollywood studio and who went on to achieve international fame as a singer,' yet was relegated to 'sing a song or two that could easily be snipped from the movie when it played in the South, where the idea of an African-American performer in anything but a subservient role in a movie with an otherwise all-white cast was unthinkable.'[196] Horne complained about treatment of black soldiers, but admitted: 'The USO got mad...from then on I was labeled a bad little Red girl.' Horne was blacklisted and censored from film industry roles after her MGM contract expired in 1950.[197] King Vidor's *Japanese War Bride* (1952) challenged the Code's interracial ban with an Asian-American marriage. Though multiethnic race relations were Asian/American rather than African-American, *Japanese War Bride* was banned in the South. Eight states and 200 cities had local censorship laws. Southern states would often cut scenes of 'ethnic' racial actors of colour from films.[198] Other independent productions eventually followed suit and dealt with interracial 'miscegenation' relations.

Revealing greater Code leeway in the post-war era, when Kazan adapted Tennessee Williams' play *A Streetcar Named Desire* in 1951, Breen allowed him to keep the play's infamous rape scene if he changed the ending. Yet, perversity and nymphomaniac tendencies of the story remained. Kazan did cut four minutes to avoid being condemned with a C (condemned) rating from the Legion of Decency. Similarly, Billy Wilder had to cut scenes from *The Seven Year Itch* (1955), and Stanley Kubrick had to cut *Spartacus* (1960), to avoid a C rating. In the end, Kazan's *A Streetcar Named Desire* received a PCA seal and the Legion gave it a B (partly objectionable) rating, although it was not a family picture. It was a box-office success, which made money with an adult audience. Likewise, in Paramount's 1951 film *Detective Story*, Breen objected to abortion, a cop killing and suicide; the word 'abortion' was deleted, yet cop killing was allowed and the film received a PCA seal and an A-II rating from the Legion despite censorable screen content. These provocative film adaptations demonstrated to the industry that filmmakers could target a specialised audience and there was no need for a film to try to please all possible viewers.

Furthermore, there were four amendments to the Code in 1951:

1. If a scene is absolutely necessary to the plot, a cop killing is okay. Abortion was a forbidden subject.

2. If the setting is a police precinct, no drugs or drug trafficking.

3. Suicide may be permitted, but must not be justified, glorified or used to defeat legal due process.

When Kazan's *Pinky* was shown in the South, it broke box-office records. Atlanta's Roxy Theatre opened the entire balcony to African-Americans. (It typically only limited a few gallery seats to black audiences.) Addressing racism, Atlanta censors insisted, 'I know this picture is going to be painful to a great many Southerners. It will make them squirm, but at the same time it will make them realise how unlovely their attitudes are.'[199] East Texas town, Marshall tried to ban the film, arresting and fining the theater owner who showed it; the PCA backed his appeal and the US Supreme Court reversed the local censor board ruling in June 1952, a week after the landmark decision on Italian film, *The Miracle*.

Foreign Films, The Miracle Decision, Breen Retires

The domestic influx of European films and reopening international markets after the war and the need for Hollywood to appeal to sophisticated viewers in foreign lands overseas, opened a debate about censorial limits on films in the US and challenged PCA censorial constraints more than ever just as a growing Cold War cultural and economic climate for American films repressed Hollywood film content. As foreign cinema markets reopened after the conflict, imported international art cinema pushed the envelope and transcended filmic boundaries of screen censorship. Hollywood censorship encountered challenges from foreign films as seen in the gritty, unvarnished portrayals of Italian neorealist cinema, such as Roberto Rossellini's *Open City* (1945, *Roma Città Aperta*), Vittorio De Sica's *The Bicycle Thief* (1948), Rossellini's *The Miracle* (1948, released in the US in

1950) and Rossellini's *Stromboli* (1950). Even Michael Powell and Emeric Pressburger's British Technicolor musical melodrama *The Red Shoes* (1948, with its doomed, scantily-clad dancers in brooding, surrealistic ballet tableaux), proved a challenge to the Production Code with its heightened cinematic realism, visual suggestion and a downbeat ending.

The influx and increased popularity in the importation of foreign films, made without the censorship of Hollywood's Production Code, eventually led to the 1952 Supreme Court *Miracle* decision, which allowed films greater First Amendment freedom of speech legal protection and ultimately contributed to an easing of PCA censorship. The influence of European films in the US was seen in the critical acclaim and censorial controversy of De Sica's *The Bicycle Thief*, Rossellini's *The Miracle* and *Stromboli*. *The Bicycle Thief* played in the World Theater art house in Manhattan as foreign films flooded urban US theatres. In an effort to expand its release and show the film in more (e.g. second run) theatres, distributors Joseph Burstyn and Arthur Mayer sought a PCA seal from Breen as MGM would release the film nationwide if it obtained a Code seal of approval. However, Breen found two scenes (one set in a bordello and another of a boy urinating on a wall) to be objectionable and insisted they be cut. The film's distributors refused and lobbied the MPAA, but MPAA head Johnson supported Breen's decision, even though the Legion rated the film a B (objectionable in part). So they released *The Bicycle Thief* without a seal to critical acclaim and it won the Academy Award for Best Foreign Film. It was the first time a film was booked without a PCA seal in a major theatre circuit since 1934. *The Bicycle Thief* was praised by critics, including Bosley Crowther of the *New York Times*, who criticised Breen and PCA censors for their refusal to issue a seal, which added to public perception that the industry's enforcement of Production Code censorship was increasingly anachronistic.

Stromboli was controversial for its star Ingrid Bergman's scandalous adulterous love affair with Roberto Rossellini, famed Italian neorealist director of *Open City* and *The Miracle*. (Although she subsequently married and had children with Rossellini, Bergman was blackballed by the industry for six years, until *Anastasia* in 1956, after she divorced him.) Censors in Memphis and other cities banned *Stromboli* (and other Bergman films), Bergman was publicly denounced by senators and congressmen in Washington as a 'disgrace' to 'American women' and a 'powerful influence for evil' indicative of a 'dangerous' 'slackening' of the 'moral code' in the

Roberto Rossellini's *The Miracle* (*L'Amore*) was a milestone for screen censorship. (University of Southern California, 1948)

xenophobic (and sexist) post-war climate of the McCarthy era. However, the script was co-written by a priest, Father Félix Morlion (uncredited) and Breen, despite his concern, admitted he was unable to stop publicity exploiting the scandal over Rossellini's film. Distributor RKO and the American Civil Liberties Union (ACLU)'s National Council on Freedom of Censorship threatened legal action to prevent theatre boycotts and the Catholic Church refused to condemn the film (after Rossellini and Bergman baptised their baby son in Rome).[200] Another Rossellini picture posed a greater challenge to screen censorship a few months later when the milestone film *The Miracle* was released in the US.

Independent distributor Joseph Burstyn opened *L'Amore* or *The Ways of Love*, an anthology film of which *The Miracle* was a part, in New York City in November 1950, after which it won the New York Film Critics Best Foreign Language Film Award in December. However, on December 23, 1950 the New York Department of Licensing Board ordered theatres to halt showings of the film, despite the film's distribution/exhibition contract being binding. *The Miracle* starred iconic Italian 'maestro' (and co-writer)

Federico Fellini and neorealist actress Anna Magnani (star of *Open City*), as a disturbed woman who is impregnated (by him) and yet believes she's the Virgin Mary. Not surprisingly, this did not play very well with Catholic audiences, censors or religious groups. The Legion of Decency condemned the film as a mockery of religious truth and an insult to religious faith and *The Miracle* was seen as another neorealism affront. Yet, many criticised the Licensing commission. It was the first case to reach the US Supreme Court since the Mutual vs. Ohio case in 1915. Two years later in *The Miracle* Decision, the court ruled against censorship to define motion pictures as a communication medium protected by free speech and found criticism of *The Miracle* to be vague and ill defined—a blow to the Legion and to regional city/state censor board laws.

In the wake of the 1948 Paramount Decision, as the classical Hollywood studio system unraveled and collapsed, federal antitrust regulation coupled with *The Miracle* Decision eliminated powerful enforcement mechanisms of the film industry's Production Code censorship. *The Miracle* Supreme Court Decision (officially, the *Joseph Burstyn, Inc. v. Wilson* case) undermined the legal basis for film censorship in the United States by granting motion pictures free speech and freedom of expression protections under the First and Fourteenth Amendments.

This was a major milestone for laying the legal groundwork to eventually overturn film censorship in the United States. By granting Hollywood motion pictures First Amendment free speech protections in 1952, *The Miracle* Decision reversed the earlier 1915 Mutual vs. Ohio decision.[201] The Decision was the first time the court had ruled that 'motion pictures are a significant medium for the communication of ideas', which was the foundation of cinematic free speech in America. The Decision ultimately rejected the legal basis of federal censorship and US government regulation, and thus significantly weakened and undercut PCA enforcement in a film industry now empowered by free speech protection. The floodgates duly opened.

For instance, director Otto Preminger defied Production Code censorship with several provocative films. His *The Moon is Blue* (1953) included the banned words 'seduce', 'virgin' and 'mistress' and was released without a PCA seal of approval. *The Man with the Golden Arm* (1955) dealt with the taboo subject of drug abuse. And Preminger's *Anatomy of a Murder* (1959) was about rape. *The Moon is Blue* was a $450,000 picture, Preminger's first independent production, released through United Artists, which Breen and the PCA insisted was objectionable because of its approach to sex and seduction. Thus, *The Moon is Blue* was not permitted a seal because of its ethos of free love. However, there was a split in the PCA and Breen was criticised for making an aesthetic decision regarding comedy. The Legion nonetheless condemned the film and it was banned in many states. Preminger recalled, 'We released it without the seal, without the approval of the Legion of Decency. That helped the picture in some places, but there were small towns where the police stood in front of the theatre and put down the names of people who went in.'[202] Yet, its star William Holden was a box-office draw and the film was a success, which effectively symbolised the death of the Code.

Fred Zinnemann's 1953 Columbia film adaptation of James Jones' acclaimed novel *From Here to Eternity* received a PCA seal and Army cooperation despite depicting an adulterous relationship between married Karen Holmes (Deborah Kerr) and Warden (Burt Lancaster), an affair between prostitute Alma/Lorene (Donna Reed) and Pruitt (Montgomery Clift) and an erotic bathing suit scene tussling around in the ocean waves. However, the Legion of Decency gave it a B rating (partially 'morally objectionable') due to its depiction of divorce. Yet, the probing Oscar-winning Best Picture did show 'compensating moral values' and regret over adultery in its downbeat finale where 'illicit' romance ends in despair.

By February 23, 1954, when Columbia Production Vice President Jerry Wald asked Twentieth Century-Fox Production chief Darryl Zanuck if he felt

Burt Lancaster and Deborah Kerr tussle in the waves in *From Here to Eternity*. (Columbia, 1953)

hampered by the Production Code, Zanuck replied, 'I have been associated, as you know, with many controversial pictures and I have had many fights with the Breen Office and with other outside censorship groups. [However] It is my belief that the Code protected me far more than it ever harmed me... It seems to me that instead of all this fuss about the Code that you should start worrying about 'outside' censorship groups both here and abroad.' He asserted: 'I defy anyone to name me ten best-selling novels or ten successful stage plays in the last ten years that could not be put on the screen because of Breen Office refusal. Frankly I do believe there were five in ten years. Of course, there were a lot of things that none of us wanted to put on the screen because they did not look like good motion picture material. But I would like to know where any of us had to pass up anything really worthwhile because of Code restrictions. ...When you can get by with *From Here to Eternity* and *A Streetcar Named Desire* and have both of them turn out to be box-office hits then I fail to see what all the furor is about. What infuriates me is the pressure groups and censorship groups both here and abroad. This is where we should carry our fight.'[203]

After two decades of enforcing Hollywood's Production Code film censorship, the PCA's chief censor Joseph Breen retired a few months later in 1954, just two years after *The Miracle* Decision. The Academy honored Breen with a lifetime achievement award at the Oscars that year, as changes in the American film industry became keenly apparent. As film historian Thomas Doherty observes: 'The controlling gaze of television, the extinction of the short film, the risky gamble on CinemaScope and the retirement of the long-serving chief of the censorious Production Code Administration— all seemed to punctuate the end of a Golden Age, a shimmering epoch when Hollywood held a monopoly over the moving image, when throwaway shorts garnished a beautiful motion picture menu, when the square-shaped motion picture screen was plenty big enough and when the moral universe projected by the medium was patrolled by a watchful sentinel.'[204] The Code and the PCA would never be the same in the absence of Breen.

4 PUSHING THE ENVELOPE: THE DEMISE OF CODE CENSORSHIP

Geoffrey Shurlock and Liberalisation of the Code in a Post-Breen Era

As Joseph Breen retired and the MPAA appointed Geoffrey Shurlock as his successor, the film industry trade journal, *Variety* reported in 1954: 'While Breen held the reins [of Hollywood PCA censorship] it was commonly referred to as the "Breen Office" or the "Breen Seal." [However] With Geoffrey Shurlock taking over, it should now theoretically become the "Shurlock Office." It'll take some getting used to after all these years.' Moreover, industry observers noted 'a decided tendency towards a broader, more casual approach' in the enforcement of the code after Breen's departure.[205]

When Geoffrey Shurlock took over the PCA that year, it was the beginning of a new era. Breen's successor, Shurlock was a moderate liberal more sympathetic to the notion of tasteful adult oriented films aimed at a specialised audience and consequently there were additional amendments to the Code just a few years later by 1956 with greater leniency toward allowing miscegenation, liquor, profanity, and a weakening of city and state censorship. Further, there were no definite film censorship standards regarding what was considered immoral and what incites violence.

In addition, women stars in Hollywood, such as Jane Russell, Rita Hayworth, Marilyn Monroe and Cyd Charisse and 'imported' European stars Sophia Loren and Gina Lollobrigida, were opening up parameters of sexuality onscreen in films which often, after much haggling, ultimately

Production Code chief censor
Geoffrey Shurlock. (University
of Southern California Regional
History Collection)

received a seal and condemned (in part) with a B rating by the Legion. Other
films were still condemned (in full) with a C rating by the Legion and refused
a Code seal. For example, in the 3-D film, *The French Line* (1953), advertising
and colour costumes emphasised star Jane Russell's breasts, so the PCA
denied the film a seal; it was released and distributed without a PCA seal
(i.e. unapproved by the Production Code censors) and was also condemned
with a C rating by the Legion.

In the absence of World War II-era censorship of screen gangsters,
films noir like Joseph H. Lewis' independent production, *The Big Combo*
(1955) enjoyed greater latitude in screen content regarding the provocative
underworld of mobsters and illegal deeds in the comparatively lax post-war
era of Production Code enforcement. Released by Allied Artists (formerly low-
budget 'poverty row' Monogram studio) after Breen's retirement, *The Big
Combo* included torture, sadistic gangsters, homosexuality and suggested
oral sex—considered shocking transgressions of the Code's moral strictures.
The *New York Times* criticised the film's brutality. Ads called *The Big Combo*
'The most startling story the screen has ever dared reveal!', but the publicity

I Don't Care What You Do To Me,
Mike—Just Do It Fast! *Kiss Me
Deadly* promoted sex and violence.
(Parklane Pictures, 1955)

was still relatively restrained compared to the film itself; rather than an implied transgressive sexual encounter, posters featured kingpin Richard Conte kissing his mistress Jean Wallace on the neck as she throws her head back in a strapless gown. In terms of censorship, 'You can't compare filmmaking of yesterday with today', Lewis insisted in retrospect. 'We had strict rules and regulations and even laws. Not that we were Puritans. It allowed us to do some of the things that you see today,' he explained. 'In our day, if we wanted to specify sex, we had to do it only by suggestion. And I think it was far more effective.' He added, 'You know if a boy and girl could start getting into the bed. Now they disrobe completely.'[206]

Another film released after Breen left the PCA, Robert Aldrich's 1955 noir *Kiss Me Deadly*, renowned for its apocalyptic atomic bomb blast, opened with a woman (Cloris Leachman) running barefoot in a trench coat with nothing on underneath on a dark night road. Her loud panting and arduous heavy breathing suggested sexual exertion. The film's publicity clamored, 'I Don't Care What You Do To Me, Mike—Just Do It Fast!' and 'Blood-Red Kisses!

White-Hot Thrills! Mickey Spillane's Latest H-Bomb!' When Mike Hammer (Ralph Meeker) picks her up and stops, a gas station attendant knowingly assumes they had sex in the car. As she flees an insane asylum, murderous hoodlums abduct and knock them out, viciously beat her to death as she screams in terror and kicks frantically while they torture her off-screen, then push them over a cliff where the car explodes. This unsettling Cold War noir universe with disturbing violence, lacking the sort of compensating moral values championed by Breen during his 20-year tenure as Production Code chief, would make the retired censor's head spin. *Kiss Me Deadly*'s provocative visceral screen content challenged the Code and explored stark lapses in PCA censorship in the new post-Breen Cold War era a decade after the war years.

However, despite greater leeway in film censorship by the mid-1950s, in 1955 there was a backlash, with investigations into the affect of sex and violence on children, the objectification and physical man-handling of women and Estes Kefauver's US congressional subcommittee on juvenile delinquency. In fact, the Legion of Decency employed the Code to strengthen itself against breakthroughs from the Left regarding censorship lapses. Typically, the PCA agreed with the Legion and local state/city censorship laws. However, that was not always the case. Preminger's 1955 film *The Man with the Golden Arm* dealt with the subject of substance addiction by a musician (Frank Sinatra) and did not receive a Code seal because it portrayed drug abuse. The film split the PCA and the Legion, which changed

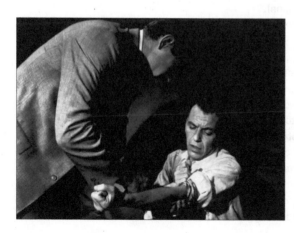

Frank Sinatra battles drug addiction in Otto Preminger's *The Man with the Golden Arm*. (Carlyle Productions, 1955)

its rating from a C (condemned) to a B (partially condemned) and United Artists released the independently produced picture despite the Legion's condemnation, without a seal and earning $4 million.

In response to the success of *The Man with the Golden Arm*, Shurlock and the PCA revamped the drug section of the Production Code, in a major revision and liberalisation of the Code itself, the following year, in 1956. That year, a committee was formed to reexamine the PCA and its appeals process. As a result, several restrictions were lifted or liberalised, a number of taboos were deleted and the Code was revised:

- Narcotics were allowed.
- Abortion was allowed (if it was suggested and condemned).
- Prostitution was allowed (if not presented in a detailed manner).
- Kidnapping was allowed.
- Childbirth was allowed (if portrayed with discretion).
- Miscegenation was allowed (if produced with discretion).

However, nonetheless, a number or restrictions remained:

- Brutality and physical violence were banned.
- Family values were upheld.
- Blasphemy was banned in religious portrayal (in capitulation to the Legion).
- Sexual perversion and venereal disease were still censorable issues.

Films such as George Stevens' *Giant* (1956), *Serenade* (1956), *Island in the Sun* (1957) and *Sayonara* (1957) were a breakthrough for depicting interracial marriage and miscegenation onscreen in the wake of the revisions in 1956 that contributed to the Code's demise. Elia Kazan tackled sexual perversion in his 1956 adaptation of Tennessee Williams' play *Baby Doll* which split the PCA and the Legion when it was given a Code seal, but was condemned by the Legion, then flopped at the box-office. 'New Kazan Movie Put On Blacklist; Catholic Legion of Decency Condemns *Baby Doll*—Film Gets Code Seal,' the *New York Times* reported.[207] The 1956 film *The Bad Seed* about a murderous child *was* given a PCA Seal despite the Code's restriction on 'pictures dealing with criminal activities in which minors participate' after a few deletions. *Peyton Place* (1957) was the first film to receive the Legion's new A-III rating following the liberalisation of the Code.

By 1957, there were further accommodations regarding film censorship. The *Roth vs. US* Supreme Court Decision (concerning the publisher of 'obscene' books and magazines) defined 'obscenity' which undermined state and municipal film censorship laws. Further, the Legion added the A-III rating ('Suitable for adults only'). In the *Roth vs. US* ruling, the Supreme Court spelled out three elements of obscenity:

1. The dominant theme appeals to prurient interest in sex.
2. It offends communication standards, i.e., the material is
    offensive to community standards regarding the
    representation of sexual matters.
3. It is without redeeming social value.

Thus, as a result, in *Roth vs. US* the Supreme Court ruled that sexually explicit content (including film content) was protected as 'free speech' by the First Amendment, unless it lacked 'redeeming social importance'.[208]

A special category, Separate Classification or 'SC' Legion rating (for certain films which required caution against wrong interpretations [later changed to A-4]) was given to Preminger's 1959 film *Anatomy of a Murder*. Starring James Stewart, with a vibrant jazz music score by Duke Ellington, *Anatomy of a Murder* involved the murder trial of an army lieutenant, a rape scene and a Catholic woman who swears on a rosary, and a script that included words with illicit sexual suggestion that challenged the Production Code, such as: rape, sperm, panties, climax and bra. However, despite, or because of, its seemingly provocative subject matter, Preminger's *Anatomy of a Murder* was a huge success, which made $5.5 million and was nominated for eight Academy Awards—Best Picture, Director, Actor, Supporting Actors, Writing, Editing, Cinematography and winning Best Soundtrack Score for Ellington. Joseph Mankiewicz's *Suddenly, Last Summer* (1959) was similarly controversial, with censorable content that violated the Code (in this case, implying homosexuality, cannibalistic murder, a psychopathic Oedipal relationship and violent sexual assault) which nonetheless received a PCA seal and an 'SC' Separate Classification rating from the Legion.

As Hollywood film censorship continued to ease, 1959 saw films that included taboo topics and featured censorable content which violated the

Code, suggesting salacious innuendo, homosexuality, pre-marital sex, teen pregnancy and sexual perversion: *Anatomy of a Murder, Suddenly, Last Summer, Some Like It Hot* (1959), *Pillow Talk* (1959), *Blue Denim* (1959), *A Summer Place* (1959), *Happy Anniversary* (1959) and *North by Northwest* (1959). Preminger's *The Moon is Blue, The Man with the Golden Arm* and *Anatomy of a Murder* set a precedent for later films that defied PCA compliance and were nonetheless box-office hits, such as Billy Wilder's *Some Like It Hot* and Alfred Hitchcock's *Psycho* (1960), which were released without a PCA seal because of their provocative content and censorable themes. In light of these post-war developments, Code enforcement was further weakened with the classical studio system's collapse—as Hollywood censorship unravelled in the 1960s.

The Final Decade of the Code: Foreign Films, Jack Valenti, Code Lapses

By the late-1950s and 1960s, a changing cultural sphere and evolving cine-matic industrial climate, a weakening classical studio system and its system of self-regulation and a legal framework favouring greater free speech protections granted to motion pictures, all contributed to a challenging production and reception climate for screen censorship. The sixties saw the collapse of the classical Hollywood studio system (in the wake of the post-war Paramount Decision in which major studios had to 'dis-integrate' by the end of 1959), thereby undermining its system of industry self-censorship and censorial enforcement by the Production Code Administration. In addition to the Paramount Decision, US Supreme Court rulings such as the landmark *Miracle* Decision granted First and Fourteenth Amendment free speech protections to film as a medium of communication (and thus ended the legal climate which had previously given censorship authority to state and local governments), thereby further undermining regulation. In *Roth v. US*, the Supreme Court ruled that sexually explicit content was protected as 'free speech' and by 1961–1965, state and federal appellate courts consistently reject efforts to censor films. Even the Legion of Decency lost strength in the 1960s and became the National Catholic Office for Motion Pictures by 1965. Eventually, the film industry's Production Code self-censorship system was finally abandoned in 1968. By the end of the decade, in the Code's place, a rating system emerged. Filmmakers still faced challenges and constraints on cinematic content, but partial nudity, sexual content and violence became accepted in Hollywood films as screen material, characters and plot developments once banned could now play central roles.

There were lapses in PCA enforcement with the end of the classical studio system, as seen in Hitchcock's *Psycho*, Elia Kazan's *Splendor in the Grass* (1961), William Wyler's *The Children's Hour* (1961), Stanley Kubrick's *Lolita* (1962) and *Dr. Strangelove* (1964), Sidney Lumet's *The Pawnbroker* (1965), Mike Nichols' *Who's Afraid of Virginia Woolf?* (1966) and *The Graduate* (1967) and Arthur Penn's *Bonnie and Clyde* (1967). The importation of international art films and edgier independent productions helped pave the way for greater latitude in Hollywood screen content, as in non-English language films like Michelangelo Antonioni's *La Notte* (1961) and *Blow-Up* (1966), Federico Fellini's *8 ½* (1963), François Truffaut's *400 Blows* (1959), Jean-Luc Godard's *Breathless* (1959) and *Weekend* (1967). Other overseas films such as De Sica's *The Bicycle Thief,* Rossellini's *The Miracle*, Akira Kurosawa's *Rashomon* (1950) and Louis Malle's *Les Amants* (*The Lovers*, 1958) dealt with adulterous liaisons, rape and other censorable topics, opening the doors for cinematic expression as international cinema movements like the French New Wave became the rage. The dawn of the 1960s was a turning point for foreign films hitting urban American theatres and downtown venues, including *Lady Chatterley's Lover* (1955, released in the US in 1959), *And God Created Woman* (1956; 1957 in US) and *Never on Sunday* (1960).

In 1959, the US Supreme Court ruled that the sympathetic portrayal of adultery in *Lady Chatterley's Lover* was not obscene and was protected by the First Amendment as free speech. The imported French film had been denied a screening license by New York state censors until the Supreme Court overturned the ban, ruling against government interference with the film's exhibition due to disapproval of an idea expressed onscreen, even regarding sexual content. Sexual affairs, a naked breast and adultery in *Les Amants* prompted the state of Ohio to ban the film as obscene, until the US Supreme Court reversed the ruling in 1968 against the Ohio theatre that exhibited the film. Roger Vadim's French film *And God Created Woman*, starring Bridget Bardot, was considered so controversial that Columbia Pictures created a subsidiary, Kingsley-International, to distribute the picture so its US release would not taint the reputation of the studio. Hollywood studios engaged in a subsidiary syndrome importing controversial/international films and creating subsidiaries to release them.

For example, United Artists released Billy Wilder's *Kiss Me, Stupid* (1964, condemned by the Legion) through its subsidiary, Lopert. MGM created subsidiary Premier to release Antonioni's British-made *Blow-Up*, released without a seal rather than cut its condemned nudity and ménage-a-trois and the film was a smash hit.

While the PCA fretted about implied homosexuality and pre-martial sex in *North by Northwest*, the US Interior Department banned filming violence on Mount Rushmore National Monument, so Hitchcock built a huge replica set, had Martin Landau's homosexual Leonard discuss his 'feminine intuition', dubbed the word 'discuss' over mistress Eva Marie Saint's line 'I never make love on an empty stomach' and ended with a train entering a tunnel to imply sexual intercourse. By November 1959, the PCA approved the basic story of Hitchcock's *Psycho* but nixed the 'incestuous relationship' between psychopathic serial killer Norman Bates (Anthony Perkins) and his mother, transvestites and showing a flushing toilet. Censors rejected the film on February 19, 1960 because the opening scene of Marion Crane (Janet Leigh) and her lover Sam Loomis (John Gavin) was 'entirely too passionate', Norman watching Marion undress was too 'sexually suggestive', and the shower sequence murder with 'a number of shots, some impressionistic, some completely realistic, of the girl's nude body' was in 'violation of the Code, which prohibits nudity "in fact or in silhouette"'. A seal was eventually issued on March 3, 1960. The Legion required three cuts (Marion removing her bra, Norman washing blood off his hands and a stabbing be shortened) before giving *Psycho* a B rating, complaining: 'The sensational use of sex and the excessive violence, which partially mar the development of the story, are considered to be entirely lacking in dramatic justification and to be highly objectionable.'[209] Hitchcock deftly avoided Code censorship by filming over 70 shots of the nude shower murder with his *Alfred Hitchcock Presents* TV crew over a week and editing a brutal 45-second stabbing montage sequence where he claimed the knife never touches the skin, breasts are not shown and chocolate syrup was used as blood. Yet violence, nudity, incest, transvestitism, serial killing, illicit sex and that flushing toilet remained in the film. *Psycho* received an X (adults only) certificate from British censors.

Warner Bros. promoted Natalie Wood and Warren Beatty's sexual attraction in Elia Kazan's 1961 *Splendor in the Grass* to show public moviegoer screen appetites demanded 'adult' cinema more than

Alfred Hitchcock
directs Janet
Leigh in a bra in
Psycho. (Shamley
Productions, 1960)

censorship pressure groups suggested. By the 1960s, Hollywood studios resisted U.S. film censorship as filmmakers competed with international art cinema with adult subject matter like Fellini's *La Dolce Vita* (1960), Jack Clayton's *Room at the Top* (1959), and Dassin's *Never on Sunday*. *Splendor in the Grass* previewed in screenings across the country with interviews for filmed television ads asking: 'Do you think children 16 or under should see *Splendor in the Grass*?', 'Did you find anything censorable in the picture?' and 'Should Hollywood attempt themes as sensitive as this one?' to gin up publicity for the film. *Variety* reported the studio was 'whipping up the intrigue...trying to implant in the public's mind the idea that this Elia Kazan entry is controversial' to sell tickets. Exploiting a lax Advertising Code, *Splendor in the Grass* ads showed a man lifting a woman 'ecstatically nuzzling' his ear (using a stock photo for 1954 film *The Barefoot Contessa*).

MPAA head Jack Valenti. (University of Southern California Regional History Collection)

Warners insisted theater exhibitors only allow adults and children over sixteen to see the film, unless accompanied by an adult.[210]

Screen censorship was further compromised when MPAA head Eric Johnston died in 1963, leaving a leadership vacuum at the organisation; his successor, Jack Valenti, was not hired until 1966, after a three-year search. By June 1966, Vincent Canby of *The Globe and Mail* called the MPAA the 'US motion picture Establishment', which 'displayed more suspicion of change than its critics deemed necessary.' He described 'new film czar' Valenti as 'examining the entire question—the philosophy—of self-censorship as represented by the Code'.[211] The Code was rapidly becoming obsolete. When *The Pawnbroker* was denied a PCA seal in 1965 because of nudity, producers appealed and the Code Review Board granted the film an exception, on the grounds of tasteful humanism (one nude scene was a prostitute, another showed naked women prisoners in a Nazi concentration camp about to die), which opened the door for screen nudity. (The Legion condemned the film, then gave it an A-III.)

As Mark Harris observes, by 1966, 'the Code's rigidity had recently begun to work against it. The influx of European films, some with nudity, that weren't produced by studios and didn't require a Code seal had created a double standard; local theatres, meeting the demands of their audiences, were increasingly willing to show movies without Code approval, as well as those that had been branded with the Catholic rating "Condemned."'[212] Moreover, Harris explains: 'The double standard didn't only apply to sex: Dated and rarely enforced Code provisions against things like "trick methods shown for concealing guns", "illegal abduction" and the depiction of a "notorious real-life criminal" who had not been punished for his crimes had turned Hollywood's rule book into a bizarre patchwork of policies, some rigorously enforced and others routinely ignored.' As Harris suggests, 'The 1965 decision to approve the nudity in *The Pawnbroker* because of the film's high quality had created an untenable loophole, suggesting that one standard existed for good films and another for ordinary films.'[213]

The Pawnbroker was followed by another provocative challenge to censorship with Mike Nichols' *Who's Afraid of Virginia Woolf?* in 1966, the first film given an A-IV rating (For Adults with Reservations) by the Legion and an SMA (Suggested for Mature Audiences) MPAA rating for 'blatant' material. Valenti liberalized the Production Code in 1966, creating a new Motion Picture Code Review Board to hear appeals, insisting it 'does

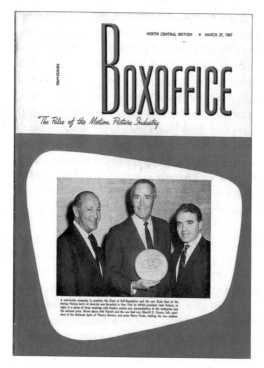

By 1967, *Boxoffice* promoted Valenti (with Fonda) and a New MPAA Seal as the Code neared its demise. (University of Southern California Regional History Collection)

not mean the floodgates are open for language or other material', as *Bonnie and Clyde* went into production. Friend and former assistant to US President Lyndon Johnson, Valenti's 1966 appointment as MPPA President was engineered by MCA studio executive Lew Wasserman to keep federal government censorship out of Hollywood and keep the PCA on a liberal track. In 1966, *Alfie*, featuring an abortion (initially denied a seal) and *Hawaii*, the first Code-approved film that depicted bare breasts, were given SMA ratings. By April 1967, revealing how much the censorship climate had changed in Hollywood, Valenti admitted, 'Personally, I think *Blow-Up* [which was denied a PCA seal] is a marvelous picture!'[214]

The Demise of the Code

The 1960s marked the end of an era for Hollywood censorship with the demise of the classical studio system old guard amid a young, rebellious 'counterculture' sexual revolution generation of 'sex, drugs and rock 'n roll' ushering a new Hollywood renaissance and a resurgence in independent production and provocative films by the end of the decade, such as *The Graduate* and *Bonnie and Clyde*. By 1967, the Code was all but dead. Arthur Penn's counterculture gangster film *Bonnie and Clyde* depicted graphic violence, allegorically criticising the Vietnam War and freewheeling sexual encounters by its unruly outlaws. Inspired by French New Wave cinema (Truffaut, Godard) and noir crime films (*Gun Crazy*, 1950), a homosexual/bisexual ménage-a-trois was omitted from the original story, but antihero Clyde (Warren Beatty) suffers sexual dysfunction and impotence. While bisexuality/homosexuality was cut, *Bonnie and Clyde* remained violent, provocative and sexually ambiguous. PCA censor Geoffrey Shurlock considered *Bonnie and Clyde* 'unacceptably brutal', 'excessively gruesome' and 'grossly animalistic'.[215]

Mike Nichols' countercultural black comedy *The Graduate* captured the rebellious, existential spirit of the sexual revolution with its depiction of an illicit sexual affair between a young college graduate, Benjamin (Dustin Hoffman) seduced by a married older woman and his parents' business partner's wife, Mrs. Robinson (Anne Bancroft), boldly defying Code censorship. Yet, according to Mark Harris, executive producer Joseph E. Levine 'didn't see the movie he expected to see. Where was all the sex?'. He wanted *The Graduate* to be more of a 'sex film' or comedy: 'How was he supposed to sell something so uncategorizable?' By late-1967, *The Graduate* 'could have gotten away with far more than it was showing', Harris observes. Nichols included a strip club scene and nude montage with a 'millisecond of skin: a blink-and-you-miss-it nipple that belonged to Anne Bancroft's body double, used by Nichols as a shock cut from Benjamin's terrified face in the scene in which Mrs. Robinson traps him in Elaine's bedroom'.[216] Bancroft, her agent Leonard Hirshan and lawyer Norma Zarky had 'contractual veto power' over whose nipple would be seen and how long it would appear onscreen.

Note that, in this case, an actress's power in post-studio system Hollywood (via her agent and lawyer; no longer 'under contract' to a studio)—not studio or government power—was key in constraining film content. Further, in a post-classical era where the Code was all but gone, greater commercialism and freedom pushed immediately towards more sex and 'poor taste'. 'There was a brouhaha,' Hoffman recalled. Producer Levine 'wanted me and Anne to be naked in the poster' for *The Graduate*. 'She was supposed to be sitting on the bed and I would have my back to the camera so you can see my ass and she's looking up at me.' Hoffman insisted: 'The reason he wanted that is that he was thinking, "All this movie's ever going to be is an art-house release and if people think there's nudity, maybe they'll come. ... [However] Anne wouldn't do it, but the one who *really* wouldn't do it was Nichols.'[217] The National Catholic Office for Motion Pictures (which replaced the Legion) 'came up with a pained endorsement' of *The Graduate*, Harris explained and declared the 'bedroom scene where Ben tries to talk with his mistress' is 'perhaps the best statement on film about how joyless an affair can be... There is no mistaking the point'.[218]

It was the final gasp of PCA censorship. The next year, after decades of screen regulation, in 1968 the Production Code was discarded and replaced with an MPAA ratings system.

The Code was finally gone.

EPILOGUE: THE POST-PCA LEGACY OF CENSORSHIP

Aftermath – The Ratings System and Legacy of the Code after the PCA

MPAA chairman Jack Valenti and studio officials created the Code and Rating Administration (CARA) nationwide system of voluntary ratings, based on a viewer's age, after years of resistance to the Production Code and courts ruled that local communities could create their own ratings system and different First Amendment standards applied to adults and minors. In 1968, the MPAA 'CARA' ratings were:

G – General Audiences.
M – Mature Audiences, parental discretion advised.
R – Restricted, 16 (changed to 17 in 1970) and above, unless accompanied by a parent or guardian.
X – Adults only, under 16 (changed to 17 in 1970) not admitted.

In 1970, M was changed to:
GP – General Audiences, parental guidance suggested under 17.

In 1972, GP was changed to:
PG – Parental Guidance suggested.

In 1984, a new MPAA rating was added as a mid-point between PG and R:

PG-13 – Parents Strongly Cautioned – some material may be inappropriate for children under 13.

In 1990, the MPAA replaced X with:

NC-17 – no children under 17 admitted (changed to 'no one 17 and under admitted' in 1996).

Geoffrey Shurlock had left the PCA by the end of 1968. By 1969, a new post-PCA Hollywood era under the ratings system—without Production Code censorship—was flourishing, as was evident in the violence, nudity, drugs, blasphemy, satanic rape/possession and sexual content in *Rosemary's Baby* (1968), *Easy Rider* (1969), *The Wild Bunch* (1969) and *Midnight Cowboy* (1969), about a male prostitute, the first (and only) X-rated film to receive three Academy Awards including a Best Picture Oscar. The provocative content of *A Clockwork Orange* (1971), *Carnal Knowledge* (1971), *The Last Picture Show* (1971), *Cabaret* (1972), *The Godfather* (1972), *The Exorcist* (1973), *The Godfather, Part II* (1974), *Texas Chainsaw Massacre* (1974), *Jaws* (1975), *The Omen* (1976) and *Taxi Driver* (1976) would have been unimaginable under the Code just a few years earlier.

Nonetheless, efforts to control film content persisted in the absence of Code censorship. By 1972, the 'voluntary' MPAA ratings system still courted controversy. 'In numerous official statements defending the rating board, MPAA president Jack Valenti has insisted that the board does nothing more than label films as to their suitability for children' with the 'purpose' of disseminating 'information that will help parents to make decisions about their children's movie going', Stephen Farber and Estelle Changas wrote in the *New York Times* in April 1972. However, 'The board actually has several secret duties in addition to classifying films. As in the days of industry censors Will Hays and Joe Breen, board members participate in re-editing films and even in reshaping scripts. In other words,' they explain, 'the board circumscribes the rights of adults as well as those of minors; it restricts the creative freedom of filmmakers and the adult audience's freedom to see what it chooses. The notorious Production Code, introduced in 1930 and used to control film content for almost four decades, has finally been abandoned, but the members of the rating board—several of whom are veterans of the Hays code office—still function as unofficial censors of American films.'[219]

Asserting that censorship persisted beneath-the-radar in a secret process reminiscent of the earlier Code era, they observed, 'We were surprised to learn that studios still submit scripts to the board and the board sends back letters threatening stiff restrictions, itemizing deletions and recommending exactly how "sensitive" scenes should be played. Many scripts are rewritten to take account of the board's objections, then are resubmitted perhaps as many as three or four times. Individual board members admitted they were harsher on scripts than on finished films; their aim was to "get out as much as we can." Films are emasculated before shooting even begins.' They noted: 'More tampering takes place after the film is completed. Approximately 50 per cent of all films in release today were first reedited at the direction of the rating board in order to make them more "suitable" for mass consumption.' After serving on the rating board for a year, Farber and Changas expressed concern that 'board members believe they are charged with the responsibility of cleaning up the screen. Although they do not represent the creative film community—or the contemporary movie audience—they feel qualified to sit in judgment on the industry.' Thus, the rating system effectively censored films: 'They used an ugly, revealing euphemism for re-editing—they called it "correcting" a film—and they often told themselves that their censored version (no matter how mutilated) played better than the original.'[220]

Films typically included far more violence than sex in the 'slay-over-lay' standard governing CARA ratings. Filmmakers often negotiated for a desired rating. *A Clockwork Orange*, originally rated X, was changed to an R rating after trimming a sex scene, yet no graphic violence was cut. *The Godfather* omitted mentioning 'Mafia' after Italian-American protests, but a bloody severed horse's head in bed remained. Washington, DC banned minors from *The Exorcist*—critics expressed surprising dismay that the film was R-rated (not X) because Warner Bros. invested $10 million and insisted it had no sexual content.[221] A great white shark devoured a naked woman at the beginning of Steven Spielberg's PG-rated blockbuster *Jaws*; *Los Angeles Times* critic Charles Champlin insisted 'the PG rating is grievously wrong and misleading... *Jaws* is too gruesome for children and likely to turn the stomach of the impressionable at any age'.[222] Martin Scorsese muted and 'de-saturated' the colour red from a bloody violent scene in *Taxi Driver* to get an R rather than an X-rating. Meanwhile, important court decisions continued to rule against censorship.[223] Georgia banned and seized a print of *Carnal Knowledge*, arresting a theatre manager, but the US Supreme Court overturned the conviction, noting display of genitals and simulated sex scenes did not constitute 'obscenity'. Federal court ruled *The Last Picture Show*, banned in Phoenix for a skinny-dipping scene, was not obscene. In 1972, the first 'pay TV' service, HBO (Home Box Office) presented uncut films soon after theatrical release. Sexuality, drugs, bisexual ménage-a-trois and abortion in *Cabaret* and *All That Jazz* (1979) and violence in *Taxi Driver* and *Raging Bull* (1980) pushed the envelope of formerly-forbidden content. Countries banned and theatres stopped showing violent *Texas Chainsaw Massacre* (originally X, cut to R) after viewers walked out; *Street Fighter* (1975) was the first film given an X for violence.

The adult-only X-rating was not trademarked by the MPAA, allowing filmmakers to self-classify their films under X. By the 1970s-1980s, rated-X became synonymous with pornography. Many theatres refused to screen (and newspapers/TV refused to advertise) X-rated films. As the X market exploded in porn houses (and on home video), pornographers exploited the X-rating with hyperbolic XXX ratings to mean 'hardcore' pornography. Influenced by the ratings system, *Deep Throat* (1972) epitomised the new trend of pornography films, which made 'porn' fashionable and part of everyday conversation.

In 1977, CARA was renamed Classification and Rating Administration. By May 1981, the *New York Times* questioned whether ratings served Hollywood or the public: 'while the ratings system stands apparently poised between the liberalism of the late-1970's and the prospect of a more restrictive climate in the 1980's', Moira Hodgson reported major CARA changes over the years, including: 'Sexual material and language that once would have earned a film an X are now the stuff of an R rating, although hard core sex still gets an X.' Further, 'X ratings which used to be conferred mostly for sex are now used to designate violence as well' and 'movies that once would have been rated PG for violence are now rated R'. Finally, 'R ratings are automatically conferred on sexually oriented language'. However, 'CARA does not hand down immutable ratings like grades on final examinations', the *Times* noted: 'Shrewd movie directors actually manipulate the system to gain the ratings which they believe will be most helpful in the marketing of their films.' Over time, different ratings had changing connotations for audiences, filmmakers and studios (not to mention those rating the films). For instance, by 1981 Hodgson explained, 'G (suitable for general audiences) is today considered box-office poison for many films on the grounds that the G can be equated with kiddie movies which arouse little interest among the majority of moviegoers'. In contrast, 'PG and R are thought to draw audiences away from their homes (and television sets) simply because moviegoers, as always, enjoy a measure of titillation... Consequently, many sophisticated filmmakers are believed to deliberately drop into their films an obscene word or two guaranteed to draw the R rating.'[224]

In the post-PCA era, sexuality, porn, violence, gore, religious and social-political commentary in films still faced controversy, even on home video.[225] By 1984, a new MPAA rating PG-13 was added after public outcry over Steven Spielberg film projects *Poltergeist* (1982), *Indiana Jones and Temple of Doom* (1984) and *Gremlins* (1984) all receiving PG ratings despite disturbing images of gore. *Red Dawn* (1984) was the first PG-13 film released. Scorsese's *The Last Temptation of Christ* (1988) faced protesters outside theatres and boycotts over its portrayal of Jesus and Mary Magdalene having a sexual relationship.[226]

In 1990, to differentiate art films from pornography, the X rating was replaced by NC-17. *Henry & June* (1990) was the first film to get an NC-17 rating. *Natural Born Killers* (1994) was rated NC-17, but cut to receive an R rating. CARA used the threat of an X or NC-17 rating to motivate filmmakers to cut objectionable material from films.[227] No NC-17 films were major box-office successes; industrial 'economic' censorship persisted as theatres and retailers refused to show/carry NC-17 films.[228] By 1995, *Los Angeles Times* critic Kenneth Turan lambasted the first NC-17 film to get a wide studio release, *Showgirls*, for its 'demeaning treatment of women' and making 'extensive nudity exquisitely boring'.[229]

Contemporary Debates about Censorship

Contemporary debates continue over issues of censorship in modern globalised film culture with changing mechanisms of reception and production, censorship by the market, debates on ideology and hegemony and censorial constraints on film content. When do 'propaganda' imperatives act as a 'censor' in certain areas of film culture? Global geopolitical and/or industrial economic considerations imposed censorial constraints. China opposed *Kundun* (1997) because it favourably portrayed the Dalai Lama, then banned the movie and filmmakers from entering the country (Disney eventually apologised to China for the film). The violence in *Saving Private Ryan* (1998) faced scrutiny and was banned in Malaysia. *Whale Rider* (2002) received a PG-13 rating because of a brief glimpse of a marijuana bong in the background, despite the film's anti-drug message. The provocative screen content in Sony's black comedy *The Interview* triggered a backlash over its portrayal of North Korea's leader: the studio faced hacking and terror threats, which prompted theatres not to show the film and disrupted its release, leading Sony to cancel its release. Sony was 'deeply saddened at this brazen effort to suppress the distribution of a movie,' the company stated on December 17, 2014. 'We stand by our filmmakers and their right to free expression.' However, 'in light of the decision by the majority of our exhibitors not to show the film,' the studio was shelving the film and scrapping its Christmas release. 'Sony wasn't standing by the movie,' *Fortune*'s Peter Elkind insisted.[230] After an uproar over the censorship of the picture, Sony later released the film online and on media streaming sites then eventually in a few theaters. (The head of Sony Pictures was subsequently ousted.)

The Motion Picture Association of America trade group protects the business interests of major US film studios—Comcast (Universal), Disney (acquiring Fox), Sony, Time Warner (Warner Bros.) and Viacom (Paramount)— and manages the US film rating system CARA with ratings partner, the National Association of Theatre Owners. Comparatively, in the post-Code era, there is greater latitude in screen content than during the constraints of the classical Hollywood era of Production Code enforcement regulating cinematic sex, nudity, violence, language, and 'compensating moral values.' There have been concerns about gun violence, animal cruelty, and smoking in films. CARA still faces controversy as critics question the arbitrary (and secretive) determination of ratings for different films. While membership is 'voluntary', all major Hollywood studios submit films to the MPAA rating board. 'Some people who do not understand the rating system blame the studios for agreeing to edit their films in return for a less restrictive rating that may mean a wider audience and heftier profits. A common argument is that editing is always "voluntary." But no filmmaker wants to cut' their film, Farber and Changas insisted. 'The board offers the filmmaker and the studio only two choices, a choice of evils: either they can accept a harsh restriction that deprives them of part of the audience they intend to reach, or they can edit their films according to the board's specifications.'[231] Unrated films are not shown in any MPAA-affiliated theatres and in many markets, viewers have little or no access to NC-17 or unrated films.[232]

More recently, however, free speech has flourished on the internet as online film/media streaming subscription services, such as Netflix and Amazon, have changed how films are distributed and consumed and make greater content available to more viewers, including unrated, NC-17 and previously unreleased movies. In a globalised digital age, films are readily available online, whether classic films challenging Production Code censorship, international art cinema, documentaries or provocative New Hollywood pictures that, in the absence of PCA regulation, defy the MPAA ratings system with increasingly bold screen content which, no doubt, would have mortified Joseph Breen. Yet, in a global era of media conglomeration and convergence, multinational corporations (which acquired major 'New Hollywood' studios) are increasingly inclined to control film content and the availability of films (and long-form dramas) to stream online. As Chuck Tryon suggests, 'Despite the promises of ubiquitous and immediate access to a wide range of media content, digital delivery has largely involved the continued efforts of major media conglomerates to develop better mechanisms for controlling when, where and how content is circulated'.[233]

Motion pictures have always been produced, distributed and exhibited in relation to a variety of constraints. Historically, film censorship has been enforced via controlling the distribution and exhibition of cinema and the films able to be released and shown to spectators in theaters. Indeed, in a modern globalised film culture, new media companies like Netflix have transformed the way we now see films, as the cinema-viewing public increasingly streams movies at home or on mobile devices rather than watching films conventionally in theaters. Moreover, like Hollywood filmmaking studios, Netflix is also producing films, as well as original long-form cinematic programs, and making global agreements to stream films and media internationally.

However, in an ever-changing global regulatory film-viewing climate, new strictures arise which affect and often constrain the ability to see and screen films. For instance, the Cannes Film Festival banned Netflix films from competition unless they screen in theaters in France first and then wait for three years before they are available to stream and be shown on Netflix. In April 2018, Farah Nayeri of the *New York Times* observed, 'Last year, two Netflix movies were in the running for the top prize. But a rule now requires all competition titles to be released in French movie theaters. France protects its film industry through a system of subsidies and regulations, and one regulation forbids cinema releases from being streamed in the country on services such as Netflix for three years.'[234] Casualties of the Cannes rule change, which banned Netflix from competition (and Netflix's boycott of 'having our films and filmmakers treated disrespectfully at the festival'), were the long awaited unveiling of Orson Welles' *The Other Side of the Wind* (unfinished when the former-Cannes jury president and Palme d'Or winner died in 1985, but recently completed in 2018 with funding from Netflix) and Alfonso Cuaron's *Roma* premiere at Cannes. In 2017, Netflix films competing at Cannes, Bong Joon-ho's *Okja* and Noah Baumbach's *The Meyerowitz Stories*, faced widespread protest from French filmmakers. Moreover, Netflix was 'unable to secure last-minute permits for one-week theatrical releases due to French media regulations.'[235] Yet, Netflix has become a major distributor and producer of independent films screened at other film festivals such as Sundance, in an era when it is increasingly difficult for films to get made and released at all and be seen. In fact, even 87-year-old French New Wave cinema auteur Jean-Luc Godard, a festival legend for 60 years, wanted to release his new film *The Image Book* on Netflix at the same time it premiered at Cannes, before any theatrical release.[236] 'I think it's a shame that a streaming service like Netflix, which makes good movies, should be absent in Cannes. Children spend their time watching movies on their smartphones and computers, and only exceptionally go to movie theaters,' Michel Abouchahla of French film trade paper *Ecran Total* admitted.[237] As films were banned from Cannes and Hollywood studios produce fewer art films, *Variety* pondered, 'With Netflix Out and Stars Absent, Will Cannes Remain Influential?...the types of films that Cannes typically celebrates—offbeat, auteur-driven meditations—are getting edged out in a business increasingly dominated by [blockbuster franchise] tentpole movies and sequels. The publicity value of launching a movie in France or selling foreign rights has begun to diminish at...[Hollywood] studios.'[238] Steven Spielberg complained: 'a lot of studios would rather just make branded tentpole guaranteed box-office hits from their inventory... than take chances on smaller films. And those smaller films that studios used to make routinely, are now going to Amazon, Hulu, and Netflix.'[239]

Nevertheless, Saudi Arabia, after closing theaters to the public since 1979, finally opened movie theaters to show the first film in 35 years,

Disney's Marvel blockbuster *Black Panther* in April 2018. Alex Ward of *Vox* reported that 'Saudi men and women will attend the screening at a swanky new theater in Riyadh featuring 500 leather seats and marble bathrooms.' Further, AMC plans to build 100 new movie theaters in 25 cities in Saudi Arabia by 2030. However, the government's Ministry of Culture insisted that films 'will be subject to censorship according to media policy standards of the Kingdom, stressing that will be in line with values and principles in place and do not contradict with Sharia Laws and moral values in the Kingdom.'[240]

In a new digital culture era, to what extent do these kinds of global exhibition constraints and regulations constitute censoring cinema? These developments regarding film distribution/exhibition and availability of films affecting cinema viewing raise new questions about film censorship in a contemporary global moving image culture. Moreover, as major media conglomerates increasingly endeavour to compete with new media companies like Netflix by pulling films and moving cinema titles to their own rival proprietary streaming outlets, movies are no longer available to be viewed. That is, media corporations control the 'circulation' of cinema by basically removing films and putting movies behind a cinema 'paywall', requiring viewers to pay additional, separate subscriptions to different companies to see films. For example, as conglomerates like Disney acquire other companies (Fox, Marvel, Pixar, Miramax, LucasFilm, BamTech, ABC, ESPN) then end deals to release films on Netflix and pull films from digital platforms to develop their own rival streaming services, it is worth considering the extent to which these developments, regarding the control of film distribution/exhibition, availability, and concentration of ownership, are related to a censoring of cinema in this growing new media environment. This is particularly the case when media companies and their films are banned, or films disappear and are not available to be seen at cinema festivals, in theaters, on DVD/Blu-ray/digital download, or to binge watch via streaming at home. Thus, ironically—as with Sony pulling *The Interview* or Cannes banning Netflix or Saudi Arabia censoring films or Disney (and other media companies) removing films from rival streaming services—in the name of theatrical viewing of films being shown (or not shown) in a movie theater or proprietary conglomerate media ownership, films are increasingly not available to be seen.

As the term 'censorship' is invoked in contemporary parlance, there are distinctions between federal censorship regulation enforced by the government, a voluntary self-censorship system enforced by the film industry as in classical Hollywood, and efforts by a studio to constrain film content to secure a desired rating or market a film internationally vis-à-vis corporate/conglomerate media ownership in a modern global film culture. While the screen censorship of Hollywood's Production Code is gone, these differing emergent kinds of film regulation amid media industry changes indicate shifting cinema distribution/exhibition practices affecting film censorship considerations in a contemporary globalised 'new media' digital era. This evolving cinematic production context raises new questions and concerns regarding the future of film/media regulatory constraints in the United States and abroad. As the film industry changes amid these emergent new media considerations, such extraordinary developments transform issues relating to film censorship, cinema distribution, exhibition, the availability of films and their censorial regulation vis-à-vis corporate industrial film/media control or international constraints regarding moving images in a global arena in the future.

NOTES

1   Peter Elkind, 'Sony Pictures: Inside the Hack of the Century, Part 3,' *Fortune*, 1 July 2015.

2   Brooks Barnes and Michael Cieply, 'Sony Drops *The Interview* Following Terrorist Threats,' *New York Times*, 18 December 2014, B1.

3   Elkind, 'Sony Pictures,' 2015.

4   Abba Kiarostami in Michel Ciment, *Film World: Interviews with cinema's leading directors*, New York: Berg Publishers, 2009, 219–220.

5   'When you dream, you dream very real. Very real. Everything seems real in a dream. You are glad to wake up, because it's so real. So, you take a dream idea...it's a nightmare—and you make it real. The audience [is] looking at a nightmare and crazy things happen...but it must be real.' Alfred Hitchcock quoted in *Hitchcock S'Explique*, French documentary, André S. Labarthe, 1965; H. E. F. Donohue, 'Remembrance of Murders Past: An Interview With Alfred Hitchcock', *New York Times*, 14 December 1969; Alfred Hitchcock, 'Master of Suspense: A Self-Analysis', *New York Times*, 1950.

6   Hollywood studios and the US government collaborated with Douglas MacArthur's Supreme Command for the Allied Powers in a postwar campaign to craft policies to influence and regulate Japan's film market during the US occupation of Japan from 1945–1952, and also censored and influenced American films. Hiroshi Kitamura, *Screening Enlightenment: Hollywood and the Cultural Reconstruction of Defeated Japan*, Ithaca: Cornell University Press, 2010.

7   Akira Kurosawa in Audie Bock, 'Kurosawa on His Innovative Cinema', *New York Times*, 4 October 1981.

8   As Kurosawa described Japanese censors: 'He explained that the word "gate" very vividly suggested to him the vagina! For these people suffering from sexual manias, anything and everything made them feel carnal desire. Because they were obscene themselves, everything seen through their obscene eyes naturally became obscene.' Akira Kurosawa, *Something Like an Autobiography*, New York: Vintage, 1983, 119.

9   After trying unsuccessfully to negotiate with the Indonesian government in Jakarta, Tanaka

conceived of *Godzilla* on the flight back to Japan. August Ragone, *Eiji Tsuburaya: Master of Monsters*, San Francisco: Chronicle Books, 2014, 33–34.

10   For further reading on regulating 'difference', see Chon Noreiga, "'Something's Missing Here!'": Homosexuality and Film Reviews during the Production Code Era, 1934–1962,' *Cinema Journal*, 30: 1, 1990, 20–41; Charlene Regester, "Black Screen/White Censors," Francis Couvares, ed., *Movie Censorship and American Culture*, Washington: Smithsonian, 1996, Amherst: University of Massachusetts Press, 2006, 159–186; Susan Courtney, *Hollywood Fantasies of Miscegenation: Spectacular Narratives of Gender and Race*, Princeton: Princeton University Press, 2004; Homay King, *Lost in Translation*, Durham, NC: Duke University Press, 2010; Ellen Scott, *Cinema Civil Rights: Regulation, Repression, and Race in the Classical Hollywood Era*, New Brunswick, NJ: Rutgers University Press, 2015; Patricia White, *Uninvited*, Bloomington: Indiana University Press, 1999; Francis Couvares, 'The Good Censor: Race, sex, and censorship in the early cinema,' *Yale Journal of Criticism*, 7: 2, 1994, 233; Shelley Stamp, 'Moral Coercion, or the Board of Censorship Ponders the Vice Question,' in *Controlling Hollywood: Censorship and Regulation in the Studio Era*, Matthew Bernstein, ed., New Brunswick, NJ: Rutgers University Press, 1999, 41–58.

11   Michael Sherry, *Gay Artists in Modern American Culture*, Chapel Hill: University of North Carolina Press, 2007, 46–47; Brian Neve, *Film and Politics in America*, New York: Routledge, 1992; David Johnson, *Lavender Scare*, Chicago: University of Chicago Press, 2004.

12   George Cukor in Peter Bogdanovich, ed., *Who the Devil Made It*, New York: Ballantine, 1997, 465.

13   For further reading on film censorship, see Leonard Leff and Jerold Simmons, *The Dame In The Kimono: Hollywood, Censorship and the Production Code from the 1920s to the 1960s*, New York: Grove, 1990, Lexington: University of Kentucky Press, 2001; Clayton R. Koppes and Gregory D. Black, *Hollywood Goes to War: How Politics, Profits and Propaganda Shaped World War II Movies*, New York: The Free Press, 1987; Gregory D. Black, *Hollywood Censored: Morality Codes, Catholics and the Movies*, Cambridge: Cambridge University Press, 1994; Francis Couvares, ed., *Movie Censorship and American Culture*, Washington: Smithsonian, 1996, Amherst: University of Massachusetts Press, 2006; Lea Jacobs, *The Wages of Sin: Censorship and the Fallen Woman Film, 1928–1942*, Madison: University of Wisconsin Press, 1991; Raymond Moley, *The Hays Office*, New York: Bobbs-Merrill, 1945; Thomas Doherty, *Pre-Code Hollywood: Sex, Immorality and Insurrection in American Cinema, 1930–1934*, New York: Columbia University Press, 1999; Richard Maltby, *Harmless Entertainment: Hollywood and the Ideology of Consensus*, Metuchen, NJ: Scarecrow, 1983; Thomas Doherty, *Hollywood's Censor: Joseph I. Breen and the Production Code Administration*, New York: Columbia University Press, 2009; Matthew Bernstein, ed., *Controlling Hollywood: Censorship and Regulation in the Studio Era*, New Brunswick, NJ: Rutgers University Press, 1999; Thomas Doherty, *Projections of War: Hollywood, American Culture and World War II*, New York: Columbia University Press, 1993; Richard B. Jewell, *The Golden Age of Cinema*, New York: Blackwell, 2007; Annette Kuhn, *Cinema, Censorship and Sexuality*, London: Routledge, 1988; Jon Lewis, *Hollywood v. Hard-Core*, New York: New York University Press, 2000; Drew Casper, *Postwar Hollywood*, Malden, MA: Blackwell, 2007; Sheri Chinen Biesen, *Blackout: World War II and the Origins of Film Noir*, Baltimore: Johns Hopkins University Press, 2005.

14   'New Films For "Screen" Machines,' *The Phonoscope*, 3.1, 1899, 15. Fatima's live 'Coochee Coochee' dance had been made famous in performances at the 1893 World's Fair and some prints of the film are dated 1894.

15   Barak Y. Orbach, 'Prizefighting and the Birth of Movie Censorship', *Yale Journal of Law and the Humanities*, 21: 2, Art 3, 2009, 251–304.

16   Ibid; for further reading, see also MPPDA Digital Archive, mppda.flinders.edu.

17   'Fight of Century, Says Jack London,' *Philadelphia Inquirer*, 2 July 1910, 10; Geoffrey Ward, *Unforgivable Blackness*, New York: Alfred Knopf, 2004, (see also Ken Burns PBS documentary); Dan Streible, *Fight Pictures—A History of Boxing and Early Cinema*, Berkeley: University of California Press, 2008; Dan Streible, 'Race and Reception of Jack Johnson Fight Films,' in Daniel Bernandi ed., *The Birth of Whiteness: Race and the Emergence of U.S. Cinema*, New Brunswick, NJ: Rutgers University Press, 1996, 170; Lee Grieveson, *Policing Cinema: Movies and Censorship in Early-Twentieth Century America*, Berkeley: University of California Press, 2004, 121–50; Barak Y. Orbach, 'The Johnson-Jeffries Fight and Censorship of Black Supremacy,' *New York University Journal of Law & Liberty*, 5: 270, 2010, 270–346; for further reading, see also MPPDA Digital Archive, mppda.flinders.edu.

18   Richard Abel, ed., *Silent Film*, New Brunswick, NJ: Rutgers University Press, 1995; Richard Abel, ed., *Encyclopedia of Early Cinema*, London: Taylor & Francis, 2005; for further reading, see also MPPDA Digital Archive, mppda.flinders.edu.

19   Mutual Film Corporation v. Industrial Commission of Ohio.

20   For more on the *Mutual vs. Ohio* Supreme Court Decision, see Clayton Koppes, 'Show Stoppers: Movie Censorship Considered as a Business Proposition', *Essays in Economic and Business History*, v. 30, 2012, 63–76; see also, Jewell.

21   Allan Dwan in Peter Bogdanovich, ed., *Who the Devil Made It*, New York: Ballantine, 1997, 81.

22   *Variety* explained: 'The instruction code is titled a "tentative draft of letter to executives of Famous Flayers-Lasky Corporation." It asserts that clean pictures have been always the aim of Famous and that the people of the United States want wholesome amusements, free from suggestive or morbid incidents. "Our dominant position in the motion picture industry has been based largely on the certainty of the fathers and mothers of the country that when they took their children to a (Paramount) picture they would find absorbing entertainment, free from all indecency", is the prelude to a subdivision of 14 points in the "code."' 'Famous Players-Lasky Ban Sex Films By Fourteen 'Don'ts' To Studio Officials... Crime and Underworld Stuff Allowable When It Serves a Moral Purpose—Illicit Love Forbidden', *Variety* LXI: 13, 18 February 1921, 46. See also, Jesse L. Lasky letter to Adolph Zukor, Academy of Motion Picture Arts and Sciences Library, Beverly Hills, California, 25 February 1921.

23   'Famous Players-Lasky Ban Sex Films By Fourteen "Don'ts"', *Variety*, 18 February 1921, 46; Jesse L. Lasky letter to Adolph Zukor, Academy of Motion Picture Arts and Sciences Library, Beverly Hills, California, 25 February 1921.

24   (Every photodrama must contain love interest and love interest involves the depiction of some form of sex attraction. The problem of the motion picture producer, therefore, is to depict wholesome love and avoid sensuality. Many scenes which are considered perfectly proper in books or on the stage become must improper when transferred to the screen.

A picture of a doubtful incident is always more shocking than a theatrical representation of the same incident and incomparably more vivid than a description by written word. Furthermore, a comparatively large number of young persons attend motion picture performances and episodes which do not shock adults when alone shock them when accompanied by children or in the presence of children. Therefore, the motion picture industry must be more careful and puritanical than publishers of books or theatrical producers.)

25   (It was justifiable to depict the white slave so long as this evil was prevalent, but the subject should now be avoided absolutely.)

26   (Illicit love affairs must not be shown in that they tend to make virtue odious and vice attractive. They compose too large a part of life to be eliminated as subjects of drama, but stories based on them must be carefully scrutinized and presented only if they can be handled with delicacy.)

27   (Long shots of naked children, like boys swimming or very young children dancing, are tolerable, but close-ups even of children should not be taken.)

28   (All close-ups of stomach dancing must be cut out absolutely.)

29   (Manhandling during love scenes is unnecessary and should be avoided.)

30   (Vice, crime and dope make ugly sordid pictures. Depiction of the actual taking of dope in any form should be avoided. Stories dealing with these subjects should not be presented unless the scenes of the underworld are merely a part of an essential conflict between good and evil.)

31   (Pictures dealing throughout with gamblers or drunkards should not be presented. The illegal and seamy side of life may certainly be shown, but it should not be the sole object of a picture.)

32   (The details of the commission of a crime should be concealed from the audience, so that no spectator could learn from the picture the method of committing a crime.)

33   (The unpleasant characters in a picture should not necessarily be identified as holders of any particular religious belief. That is, unless it is necessary to the story, as in 'The Merchant of Venice', they should not be identified as either Jews, or Roman Catholics, or Episcopalians, etc.)

34   (Scenes showing, for example, the crucifix kicked about or pages torn from the Bible should be eliminated.)

35   (Salaciousness is apt to creep into a picture by way of comedy business; winks, gestures and postures. Such comedy must be rigorously avoided.)

36   (Close-ups of bloody faces or wounds showing dripping blood are unnecessarily horrible and ought not to be shown.)

37   (Titles, stills and advertising matter which attempt to attract the public by suggesting that the picture will show vice must be avoided.)

38   *Variety* emphasised that Lasky, in 'discussing the "cleaning house" issue, wished to impress this was in no manner a direct influence brought to bear by the recent agitation in favor of eliminating "sex stuff." He declared that it was entirely of their own volition.' Lasky 'denied' the 'cleaning up' was 'attributed' to a 'recent conference' with *Christian Herald* editor Charles M. Sheldon and Gabriel L. Hess of the Censorship Committee of the National Association. 'Mr. Lasky said Mr. Sheldon told him that in but one picture had he (Sheldon)

found an element of objection. This was in *Idols of Clay*, The *Christian Herald* has a reputed circulation of over 600,000, with more readers. Mr. Lasky declared that Mr. Sheldon was not in favor of censorship.' *Variety*, 18 February 1921, 46.

39   These National Association of the Motion Picture Industry 'Thirteen Points' (shown below) were distinct and a bit different from, yet clearly influenced by, Lasky's 'Fourteen Points' (as shown above in Box 1). 'Producers Take Drastic Step to Assure 100 Per Cent. Clean Screen Productions', *Moving Picture World*, 19 March 1921, 240–241. 'National Association of the Motion Picture Industry reaffirms its emphatic protest against the production, distribution and exhibition of all motion pictures which are obscene, salacious, indecent and immoral and...while the creators of the art of the motion picture must in no way be hampered or prohibited from depicting honestly and clearly life as it is, to the end that this art may not be hindered in its movement toward the dignity of other arts, the motion picture should not be prostituted to a use or as a means toward arousing bawdy emotions or pandering a salacious curiosity, or in any other manner injurious to public welfare and...to the end that the motion picture be held in that high plane which it has already attained...'

Thirteen Points

...filmmakers 'refrain' from producing motion pictures:

1. which emphasize and exaggerate sex appeal or depict scenes therein exploiting interest in sex in an improper or suggestive form or manner;

2. based upon white slavery or commercialized vice or scenes showing the procurement of women or any of the activities attendant upon this traffic;

3. Thematically making prominent an illicit love affair which tends to make virtue odious and vice attractive;

4. with scenes which exhibit nakedness or persons scantily dressed, particularly suggestive bedroom and bathroom scenes and scenes of inciting dances;

5. with scenes which unnecessarily prolong expressions or demonstrations of passionate love;

6. Predominantly concerned with the underworld or vice and crime and like scenes, unless the scenes are part of an essential conflict between good and evil;

7. of stories which make drunkenness and gambling attractive or with scenes which show the use of narcotics and other unnatural practices dangerous to social morality;

8. of stories and scenes which may instruct the morally feeble in methods of committing crime or by cumulative processes emphasize crime and the commission of crime;

9. of stories or scenes which ridicule or deprecate public officials, officers of the law, the United States Army, the United States Navy or other governmental authority, or which tend to weaken the authority of the law;

10. of stories or with scenes or incidents which offend the religious belief of any person, creed or sect or ridicule ministers, priests, rabbis, or recognized leaders of any religious sect and also which are disrespectful to objects or symbols used in connection with any religion;

11. of stories or with scenes which unduly emphasize bloodshed and violence without justification in the structure of the story;

12. of stories or with scenes which are vulgar and portray improper gestures, posturings and attitudes;

13. with salacious titles and subtitles in connection with their presentation or exhibition and the use of salacious advertising matter, photographs and lithographs.

40 Significantly, the Federal Trade Commission charged Famous Players-Lasky (later, Paramount) with monopolising first-run exhibition by August 1921, which raised the threat of the Senate Judiciary Committee conducting investigations of the motion picture industry's political activity. The National Association of the Motion Picture Industry, headed by William A. Brady, would be replaced by the Motion Picture Producers and Distributors of America in 1922. For further reading, see MPPDA Digital Archive, mppda.flinders.edu.

41 By 1922, many states, legislatures and local municipalities still threatened to impose censorship on films.

42 See Jewell, Jacobs, Doherty.

43 Will Hays, *MPAA/MPPDA/PCA File*, Academy of Motion Picture Arts and Sciences Library, Beverly Hills, California, 1 January 1925; MPPDA Digital Archive, https://mppda.flinders. edu.au/records/242.

44 John Trumpbour, *Selling Hollywood to the World: US and European Struggles for Mastery of the Global Film Industry, 1920–1950*, New York: Cambridge University Press, 2002, 4.

45 Hays described 'The Formula' thus: 'Word about what is being done in connection with the the effort for which we have been striving so hard is... proving that the prevalent type of picture shall not become similar to the prevalent type of book and play and this whole matter is going forward. I will explain to you frankly just what the situation is – If a member company finds a book or play which they believe is not suitable for production, without being in restraint of trade, that is sent here and we send it to the member companies; we tell the other members in the Association that that is not fit for filming and the other members agree not to film it. Some 160 prevalent books and plays – best sellers – have been kept from the screen, with book and play rights of two or three million dollars. There is a realization that much that may be printed in books and shown on the stage cannot be made a proper subject for pictures.' Will Hays, *MPAA/MPPDA/PCA File*, Academy of Motion Picture Arts and Sciences Library, Beverly Hills, California, 1 January 1925; MPPDA Digital Archive, https://mppda.flinders.edu.au/records/242. See also Richard Maltby, 'To Prevent the Prevalent Type of Book: Censorship and Adaptation in Hollywood, 1924–1934', *American Quarterly*, 44.4, 1992, 561; Jewell, *The Golden Age of Cinema*; Gregory Black, 'Hollywood Censored: The Production Code Administration and the Hollywood Film Industry, 1930–1940', *Film History*, 3.3, 1989, 167–189.

46 *MPAA/MPPDA/PCA File*, Academy of Motion Picture Arts and Sciences Library, Beverly Hills, California, 1927. See also MPPDA Digital Archive, mppda.flinders.edu.

47 When Jason Joy left the SRC to join Fox Film Corp. as a studio executive in June 1932, Will Hays hired James Wingate to run the SRC, then made a deal with Fox in August 1933 to loan Joy to the MPPDA for a year. Although Wingate was SRC director, Joseph Breen effectively ran SRC operations. Breen was soon hired as director when the MPPDA established the Production Code Administration (PCA) in June 1934. (Basically, the SRC was a precursor to the PCA during this late 1920s-early 1930s period.) For further reading, see Jacobs, *The Wages of Sin*; Walsh, *Sin and Censorship*, 66–74.

48 Daniel A. Lord, *Played By Ear: The Autobiography of Daniel A. Lord, S. J.*, Chicago: Loyola University Press, 1955.

49 'The Motion Picture Production Code', published 31 March 1930, reprinted in Richard Maltby, *Hollywood Cinema*, Oxford: Blackwell, 2003, 593–597. For further reading, see MPPDA Digital Archive, mppda.flinders.edu.

50 'The Motion Picture Production Code', *MPAA/MPPDA/PCA File*, Academy of Motion Picture Arts and Sciences Library, Beverly Hills, California, 31 March 1930; MPPDA Digital Archive, mppda.flinders.edu.

51 Thomas Doherty, 'The Code Before "Da Vinci"', *Washington Post*, May 20, 2006.

52 'The Motion Picture Production Code', *MPAA/MPPDA/PCA File*, Academy of Motion Picture Arts and Sciences Library, Beverly Hills, California, 31 March 1930; MPPDA Digital Archive, mppda.flinders.edu.

53 Censors were enabled by a legal climate for censorship which, as we have seen, denied motion pictures First Amendment free speech protections given to other media such as the press.

54 A Code to Govern the Making of Talking, Synchronized and Silent Motion Pictures Formulated by The Association of Motion Picture Producers, Inc. and The Motion Picture Producers and Distributors of America, Inc., March 1930. If motion pictures present stories that will affect lives for the better, they can become the most powerful force for the improvement of mankind. 'The Motion Picture Production Code', *MPAA/MPPDA/PCA File*, Academy of Motion Picture Arts and Sciences Library, Beverly Hills, California, 31 March 1930; MPPDA Digital Archive, mppda.flinders.edu.

55 'The Motion Picture Production Code', *MPAA/MPPDA/PCA File*, Academy of Motion Picture Arts and Sciences Library, Beverly Hills, California, 31 March 1930; MPPDA Digital Archive, mppda.flinders.edu. A November 1, 1939 Code addendum noted words political censor boards banned—in England: 'Bum, Bloody, Cissy/Sissy, Gigolo, Punk, Sex appeal, Sex life, Shag, Shyster'; in the US/Canada: '"Stick 'em up", Poisons (specific names of).'

56 'Advertising Code of Ethics', *Film Daily Year Book*, New York: The Film Daily, 1931, 663.

57 See Doherty; Jewell; Leff and Simmons; Biesen.

58 'There have been some pictures which in theme, in my opinion, did not comply with the spirit of the code.' He emphasised that the 'ultimate solution' to the 'difficulty... lies with the studios themselves'. As Hays explained, 'These men are under great pressure. If they are right in any given case, the Code enforcement facilities afford means to establish the correctness of their position. Our duty is first to call attention to the probable error; discuss the matter with the studio involved; apply to such discussion the broad knowledge which you have of the general situation; to insist upon avoiding the mistake if you believe you are right; and then failing to agree, to let the matter be submitted to the provided Jury here and then appeal to the Board in New York.' Will Hays, MPPDA memo, 20 August 1932, MPPDA Digital Archive, https://mppda.flinders.edu.au/records/844

59 Ibid.

60 'A few of the situations in some recent pictures will go far toward convincing a large body of public opinion that motion picture production has admitted it cannot fabricate entertainment except with 'damaged goods.'...The mistakes that are being made, though very few in number and entirely overshadowed by the great accomplishment.' Ibid.

61 Ibid.

62 *MPAA/MPPDA/PCA File*, Academy of Motion Picture Arts and Sciences Library, Beverly Hills,

California, 1934; American Film Institute (AFI), 1934; Lea Jacobs, 'The Censorship of the Blonde Venus', *Cinema Journal*, 27, 1988, 21–31.

63   Jason Joy, *MPAA/MPPDA/PCA File*, Academy of Motion Picture Arts and Sciences Library, Beverly Hills, California, 1 September 1932. MPPDA Digital Archive – Record #855, http://mppda.flinders.edu.au/records/855

64   Will Hays, Joseph I. Breen, *MPAA/MPPDA/PCA File*, Academy of Motion Picture Arts and Sciences Library, Beverly Hills, California, 31 March 1931, 9 May 1935. MPPDA Digital Archive – Record #768, #1122, http://mppda.flinders.edu.au/records/768 , http://mppda.flinders.edu.au/records/1122

65   Rudolph Arnheim quoted in Marilyn Yaquinto, *Pump 'Em Full of Lead: A Look at Gangsters on Film*, New York: Twayne, 1998, 20.

66   Darryl Zanuck, letter to Jason Joy, *MPAA/MPPDA/PCA File*, Academy of Motion Picture Arts and Sciences Library, Beverly Hills, California, January 6, 1931.

67   Howard Hawks in Joseph McBride, ed., *Hawks on Hawks*, Lexington: The University of Kentucky Press, 2013, 53. (Drawn from interviews in the 1970s.)

68   Marlene Dietrich interviewed by William Mooring, *London Film Weekly*, 1935, in MPPDA Digital Archive, mppda.flinders.edu.au/records/2458.

69   James M. Cain quoted in David Hanna, 'Hays Censors Rile Jim Cain', *Daily News* (Los Angeles), 14 February 1944, 11–13.

70   Will Hays, *MPAA/MPPDA/PCA File*, Academy of Motion Picture Arts and Sciences Library, Beverly Hills, California, 22 March-4 September 1934. Joseph I. Breen, *MPAA/MPPDA/PCA File*, Academy of Motion Picture Arts and Sciences Library, Beverly Hills, California, 9 March-21 April 1934.

71   As early as September 1, 1924, MPPDA censors claimed 'movies are an adult entertainment, only 12.5% of audience is under 16' and thus encouraged children's matinees and the New York legislature allowing children under 16 into theatres to attend movies unaccompanied by an adult. See MPPDA Digital Archive, mppda.flinders.edu.au/records/182.

72   'Church Tightens On Pix', *Variety*, 11 December 1935, 3; 'Catholics Approve Two Debated Films', *New York Times*, 6 July 1936. For further reading on the Legion of Decency ratings, see Walsh, *Sin and Censorship*, 130.

73   The Legion added the A3 classification after a 1957 Vatican conference in Havana. For further reading, see Andrew Quicke, 'The Era of Censorship (1930–1967)', in *The Routledge Companion to Religion and Film*, John Lyden, ed., 2009, reprinted by New York: Taylor and Francis-Routledge, 2010, 32–51. *Peyton Place* (1957) received the first A-III rating.

74   For further reading, see 'Religion: Legion of Decency', *Time*, 11 June 1934.

75   'The Motion Picture Production Code' (March 1930), reprinted in Terry Ramsaye, 'What the Production Code Really Means,' *Motion Picture Herald*, 11 August 1934, 10–13.

76   Raymond Moley, *The Hays Office*, New York: Bobbs Merrill, 1945, 77–82.

77   Leff and Simmons, *The Dame in The Kimono*, 57.

78   It is worth noting that the role of West's lover, Chinese nightclub owner, Chan Lo was played by a non-Asian actor Harold Huber in 'yellowface'.

79   Will Hays and Joseph I. Breen, *MPAA/MPPDA/PCA File*, Academy of Motion Picture Arts and Sciences Library, Beverly Hills, California, July 1935-February 1936; AFI, 1936; Ramona Curry, 'Mae West as Censored Commodity: The Case of *Klondike Annie*', *Cinema Journal*,

31.1, 1991, 57–85.

80 *MPAA/MPPDA/PCA File*, Academy of Motion Picture Arts and Sciences Library, Beverly Hills, California, February-May 1936; AFI; Curry, 'Mae West as Censored', 57–85.

81 George Cukor in Peter, Bogdanovich, ed., *Who the Devil Made It*, New York: Ballantine, 1997, 465.

82 See Thomas Doherty; Richard Jewell.

83 David O. Selznick Archive, Harry Ransom Humanities Research Center, University of Texas at Austin, September 1935; see also Rudy Behlmer, ed., *Memo From David O. Selznick*, New York: Viking Press, 1972, 78–79.

84 Michael Balcon in *Motion Picture Daily*, 20 April 1935.

85 Bruce Allan, 'British Take Critical View of Code Talks: Some Editors Satirical On U.S. Film Morals', *Motion Picture Daily*, 16 May 1935, 1, 4.

86 Sheri Chinen Biesen, *Blackout: World War II and the Origins of Film Noir*, Baltimore: Johns Hopkins University Press, 2005, 1–5; chapter 3–4.

87 *Gone With the Wind* Amendment, *MPAA/MPPDA/PCA File*, Academy of Motion Picture Arts and Sciences Library, Beverly Hills, California, 1 November 1939. MPPDA Digital Archive – Record #1207, http://mppda.flinders.edu.au/records/1207 (The MPPDA board denied Selznick was given special treatment to accommodate 'damn' in the film; some sources, such as Aljean Harmetz' *On the Road to Tara* [New York: Abrams, 1996], note he paid a $5,000 fine.)

88 David O. Selznick Archive, Harry Ransom Humanities Research Center (HRC), University of Texas at Austin, 6 September 1939; see also Behlmer, *Memo From David O. Selznick*, , 275–276.

89 Ibid.

90 Selznick Archive, HRC, UT-Austin, 27 February 1940; Behlmer, *Memo From David O. Selznick*, 286–287.

91 Arthur Houghton, *MPAA/MPPDA/PCA File*, Academy of Motion Picture Arts and Sciences Library, Beverly Hills, California, 28 July 1938. MPPDA Digital Archive – Record #1189, http://mppda.flinders.edu.au/records/1189

92 Joseph I. Breen, *MPAA/MPPDA/PCA File*, Academy of Motion Picture Arts and Sciences Library, Beverly Hills, California, 18 April 1938. See also Rudy Behlmer, *Inside Warner Bros. (1935–1951)*, New York: Viking Penguin, 1985, 118–119.

93 Robert Lord to Hal Wallis, USC Warner Bros. Archive, University of Southern California, Los Angeles, California, 20 December 1939. See also Behlmer, *Inside Warner Bros.*, 119.

94 Joseph I. Breen, *MPAA/MPPDA/PCA File*, Academy of Motion Picture Arts and Sciences Library, Beverly Hills, California, 22 April 1941. See also Behlmer, *Inside Warner Bros.*, 132.

95 Will Hays, *MPAA/MPPDA/PCA File*, Academy of Motion Picture Arts and Sciences Library, Beverly Hills, California, 31 March 1931. MPPDA Digital Archive – Record #768, http://mppda.flinders.edu.au/records/768

96 Joseph I. Breen, *MPAA/MPPDA/PCA File*, Academy of Motion Picture Arts and Sciences Library, Beverly Hills, California, 9 May 1935. MPPDA Digital Archive – Record #1122, http://mppda.flinders.edu.au/records/1122

97 Joseph I. Breen, *MPAA/MPPDA/PCA File*, Academy of Motion Picture Arts and Sciences Library, Beverly Hills, California, 24 August 1936. See also Behlmer, *Inside Warner Bros.*,

31–32.

98   Joseph I. Breen, *MPAA/MPPDA/PCA File*, Academy of Motion Picture Arts and Sciences Library, Beverly Hills, California, 19 January 1938. See also Rudy Behlmer, *Inside Warner Bros.*, 66–67.

99   See also, Thomas Schatz, *Hollywood Genres*, New York: McGraw-Hill, 1981; Thomas Schatz, *Boom and Bust: American Cinema in the 1940s*, New York: Scribners, 1997; Thomas Schatz, *The Genius of the System*, New York: Pantheon, 1988, 1996.

100   Joseph I. Breen, *MPAA/MPPDA/PCA File*, Academy of Motion Picture Arts and Sciences Library, Beverly Hills, California, 15 June 1938–6 September 1939. MPPDA Digital Archive – Record #1208, http://mppda.flinders.edu.au/records/1208

101   Ibid.

102   BBFC added the 'H' Horror rating in 1932 after London and Manchester City Councils barred children from seeing *Frankenstein* (1931), even after the monster's drowning murder of a young girl was cut from the film. The BBFC typically rated films either 'U' Universal viewing or 'A' Adult advisory (unsuitable for children) categories. In 1938 even Walt Disney's *Snow White and The Seven Dwarfs* was rated A (Adult viewing) despite cuts (and years later was even cut for a U rating in 1964). Although the BBFC did not have a 'Code' equivalent to Hollywood, they classified films and had 43 grounds for deletion, in which cuts were required in order to receive a certificate:

1. Indecorous, ambiguous and irreverent titles and subtitles

2. Cruelty to animals

3. The irreverent treatment of sacred subjects

4. Drunken scenes carried to excess

5. Vulgar accessories in the staging

6. The modus operandi of criminals

7. Cruelty to young infants and excessive cruelty and torture to adults, especially women

8. Unnecessary exhibition of under-clothing

9. The exhibition of profuse bleeding

10. Nude figures

11. Offensive vulgarity and impropriety in conduct and dress

12. Indecorous dancing

13. Excessively passionate love scenes

14. Bathing scenes passing the limits of propriety

15. References to controversial politics

16. Relations of capital and labour

17. Scenes tending to disparage public characters and institutions

18. Realistic horrors of warfare

19. Scenes and incidents calculated to afford information to the enemy

20. Incidents having a tendency to disparage our Allies

21. Scenes holding up the King's uniform to contempt or ridicule

22. Subjects dealing with India, in which British Officers are seen in an odious light and otherwise attempting to suggest the disloyalty of British Officers, Native States or bringing into disrepute British prestige in the Empire

23. The exploitation of tragic incidents of the war

24. Gruesome murders and strangulation scenes

25. Executions

26. The effects of vitriol throwing

27. The drug habit, e.g. opium, morphia, cocaine, etc.

28. Subjects dealing with White Slave traffic

29. Subjects dealing with premeditated seduction of girls

30. 'First Night' scenes

31. Scenes suggestive of immorality

32. Indelicate sexual situations

33. Situations accentuating delicate marital relations

34. Men and women in bed together

35. Illicit relationships

36. Prostitution and procuration

37. Incidents indicating the actual perpetration of criminal assaults on women

38. Scenes depicting the effect of venereal disease, inherited or acquired

39. Incidents suggestive of incestuous relations

40. Themes and references relative to 'race suicide'

41. Confinements

42. Scenes laid in disorderly houses

43. Materialisation of the conventional figure of Christ.

103 Joseph I. Breen, *MPAA/MPPDA/PCA File*, Academy of Motion Picture Arts and Sciences Library, Beverly Hills, California, 8 September 1938–6 September 1939. MPPDA Digital Archive – Record #1208, http://mppda.flinders.edu.au/records/1208

104 Biesen, *Blackout*, 1–5.

105 Thomas Doherty, *Hollywood and Hitler, 1933–1939*, New York: Columbia University Press, 2013, 84.

106 For further reading, see Doherty, *Hollywood and Hitler*; Steven Alan Carr, 'Inside the Chicago Exhibition of *Inside Nazi Germany* (RKO, 1938)', Society for Cinema and Media Studies, 2017.

107 From a Board of Directors resolution 'amplifying' the Production Code, whereby: 'The record, particularly in recent months, abundantly proves that the industry faces a serious emergency on account of the efforts being made to use the entertainment screen for purposes of political controversy and for the advancement of alien political philosophies. Any such use of the screen would seriously jeopardize the industry's prosperity and the popularity of the motion picture theatre. It might also result in a condition in which the entertainment industry would find itself aligned with forces inimical to the progress and tranquility of the national life.' Martin Quigley memo to Will Hays, 11 July 1938, MPPDA Digital Archive – Record #1216, http://mppda.flinders.edu.au/records/1216

108 'Newsreels to Huddle on Nazi Outrages', *Film Daily*, 17 November 1938; 19 November 1938 MPPDA memos, MPPDA Digital Archive – Record #1183, #2911, http://mppda.flinders.edu.au/records/2911

109 Joseph I. Breen, *MPAA/MPPDA/PCA File*, Academy of Motion Picture Arts and Sciences Library, Beverly Hills, California, 30 December 1938.

110 Karl Lischka, *MPAA/MPPDA/PCA File*, Academy of Motion Picture Arts and Sciences Library,

Beverly Hills, California, 22 January 1939. See also, Steven J. Ross, 'Confessions of a Nazi Spy: Warner Bros., Anti-Fascism and the Politicization of Hollywood', Warners' War: Politics, Pop Culture and Propaganda In Wartime Hollywood, Martin Kaplan and Johanna Blakley, eds, Norman Lear Center Press, University of Southern California, Los Angeles, 2004, 48–59.

111   Edward G. Robinson quoted in Bosley Crowther, 'Little Caesar Waits His Chance', New York Times, 22 January 1939. The New York Times' Crowther argued former screen gangster Robinson would like to do a film with political commentary standing up to fascism and 'has no desire to reinvest old ghosts. He is through with gangster pictures, as most every one except the C-producers are. He would like to go on now and tackle the more fearsome ogres which confront the world. And although there is no immediate prospect of the Warners permitting him to appear in an outright anti-fascist picture, he would if he had his way… It has been just exactly eight years since Little Caesar blazed his chilling way across half the motion picture screens in this country and thereby earned for Edward G. Robinson not only a lasting sobriquet but also a reputation as one of the toughest guys in the world.' In insightfully commenting on the end of Prohibition and evolution of the Hollywood gangster genre after facing screen censorship and adapting to adopt more socially realist topicality onscreen amid society's concern shifting from crime menace to the war abroad, it encouraged Robinson's desire to hang up his gangster shoes and champion fighting for the war effort. Concluding, 'what was then a terrifying and sinister social problem—the menace of gang rule—has since been effectively submerged while greater problems have risen to challenge man. Al Capone has been stored away in prison and the old mobs have either been liquidated or retired', noting Robinson's 'subsequent screen impersonations were not fashioned to detract from this fame and it soon became also embarrassing for Mr. Robinson to appear abroad. People instinctively suspected him and cautiously steered clear lest that inevitable hail of bullets should suddenly rattle from a swiftly passing car… Only Little Caesar is as great as he ever was and—ably represented by his mouthpiece, Mr. R.—pleads guilty to a desire to change his territory and go on fighting.'

112   Blind Alley memos, MPAA/MPPDA/PCA File, Academy of Motion Picture Arts and Sciences Library, Beverly Hills, California, 1935–1939.

113   Ibid.

114   Joseph I. Breen, MPAA/MPPDA/PCA File, Academy of Motion Picture Arts and Sciences Library, Beverly Hills, California, 7 May-24 July 1940.

115   Crowther, 'Little Caesar', New York Times, 22 January 1939.

116   Ibid.

117   'Chaplin is Called for Movie Inquiry: Senators Will Ask Inquiry on The Great Dictator', New York Times, 14 September 1941, 41.

118   Variety, 25 June 1941, 4. Black, Hollywood Censored, 1994, 292. Joseph I. Breen, MPAA/MPPDA/PCA File, Academy of Motion Picture Arts and Sciences Library, Beverly Hills, California, March 25, 1941. Richard B. Jewell and Vernon Harbin, The RKO Story, London: Arlington Press, 1982, 141. Leff and Simmons, The Dame In The Kimono, 110, 121.

119   Joseph I. Breen, MPAA/MPPDA/PCA File, Academy of Motion Picture Arts and Sciences Library, Beverly Hills, California, December 1940.

120   Joseph I. Breen, MPAA/MPPDA/PCA File, Academy of Motion Picture Arts and Sciences

Library, Beverly Hills, California, March 1941.

121 *Variety*, February 1943. USC Press Book Collection, University of Southern California, Los Angeles, California, 1943; AFI; *MPAA/MPPDA/PCA File*, Academy of Motion Picture Arts and Sciences Library, Beverly Hills, California, 1943.

122 John Morton Blum, *V Was for Victory: Politics and American Culture During World War II*, San Diego: Harcourt Brace Jovanovich, 1976, 31. Allan Winkler, *The Politics of Propaganda: The Office of War Information, 1942–1945*, New Haven: Yale University Press, 1978, 36.

123 Clayton R. Koppes and Gregory D. Black, *Hollywood Goes to War*, New York: The Free Press, 1987, viii, 113, 324–328.

124 Koppes and Black, 88.

125 Jewell, *Golden Age of Cinema*; Biesen, *Blackout*; See also Aljean Harmetz, *Round Up the Usual Suspects: The Making of Casablanca*, New York: Hyperion, 1992.

126 Fred Stanley, 'Hollywood Peeks Into the Future', *New York Times*, 21 February 1943.

127 Lowell Mellett, 1942, in *1944 Appropriation Hearings*, 937–940, quoted in Cedric Larson, 'The Domestic Motion Picture Work of the Office of War Information', *Hollywood Quarterly*, 3.4, 1948, 440.

128 Mellett, 1942, quoted in Larson, 440.

129 Mellett, 1943, quoted in Larson, 441.

130 Walter Wanger, 1943, quoted in Larson, 441.

131 Fred Stanley, 'News From Hollywood', *New York Times*, 21 March 1944.

132 Fred Stanley, 'Hollywood Turns To "Hate" Films: Government Lifts Ban on Showing Jap Brutality—Various Other Matters', *New York Times*, 6 February 1944. For further reading, see Mark Harris, *Five Came Back: A Story of Hollywood and the Second World War*, New York: Penguin, 2014; Koppes and Black; Biesen, *Blackout*; Doherty, *Projections of War*.

133 By omitting the American men lost in the battle.

134 See Harris, 2014.

135 Geoffrey Shurlock, *MPAA/MPPDA/PCA File*, Academy of Motion Picture Arts and Sciences Library, Beverly Hills, California, October 1941-January 1942.

136 USC Press Book Collection, University of Southern California, Los Angeles, California, 1942.

137 *MPAA/MPPDA/PCA File*, Academy of Motion Picture Arts and Sciences Library, Beverly Hills, California, 23 June 1942.

138 Joseph I. Breen, *MPAA/MPPDA/PCA File*, Academy of Motion Picture Arts and Sciences Library, Beverly Hills, California, 21 May 1942. See also Behlmer, *Inside Warner Bros.*, 207–208.

139 Joseph I. Breen, *MPAA/MPPDA/PCA File*, Academy of Motion Picture Arts and Sciences Library, Beverly Hills, California, 26 September-October 1944.

140 Leff and Simmons, *Dame in the Kimono*, 125–126.

141 Fred Stanley, 'Hollywood Crime and Romance', *New York Times*, 19 November 1944. For further reading on wartime films noir, censorship and the 'red meat' crime cycle, see also Biesen, *Blackout*.

142 Stanley, 'Hollywood Crime and Romance', 19 November 1944. See also Sheri Chinen Biesen, 'Censorship, Film Noir and *Double Indemnity*', *Film & History*, 25: 1–2, 1995, 40–52; Richard B. Jewell, *The Golden Age of Cinema*, Malden, MA: Blackwell, 2007; Schatz, *Boom and Bust*, 204–206, 232–239.

143 Philip Scheuer, 'Film History Made by *Double Indemnity*,' *Los Angeles Times*, 6 August 1944, 1, 3.

144 '*Double Indemnity* Drama of Knockout Proportions,' *Hollywood Reporter*, 24 April 1944.

145 Alfred Hitchcock quoted in *Hitchcock S'Explique*, French documentary, André S. Labarthe, 1965.

146 Joseph I. Breen, *MPAA/MPPDA/PCA File*, Academy of Motion Picture Arts and Sciences Library, Beverly Hills, California, 3 September-December 1943.

147 USC Press Book and Universal Collections, University of Southern California, Los Angeles, California, 1944.

148 James M. Cain quoted in Lloyd Shearer, 'Crime Certainly Pays on the Screen: The growing crop of homicidal films poses questions for psychologists and producers', *New York Times*, 8 August 1945.

149 *MPAA/MPPDA/PCA File*, Academy of Motion Picture Arts and Sciences Library, Beverly Hills, California, September-December 1944.

150 USC, AFI, 1945–1946. For further reading, see Matthew Bernstein, 'A Tale of Three Cities: The Banning of *Scarlet Street*', *Cinema Journal*, 35.1, 1995, 27–52. Basically, Universal and Diana Productions sued the city of Atlanta, claiming that the state censor did not have the authority to ban the film and that only the entire state Board of Censors, who tied on their vote, could make such a decision. Georgia's lower court demurred judgment in April 1946, while the film was still in its first run. The city of Atlanta appealed to the state Supreme Court, who reversed the demurrer on a legal technicality in September 1946.

151 Bernstein, 'A Tale of Three Cities: The Banning of Scarlet Street', in Bernstein, *Controlling Hollywood*, 161.

152 Stanley, 'Hollywood Crime and Romance'; Leff and Simmons, 130–135; Biesen, *Blackout*, 1–5, 115–121; Frank Krutnik, *In a Lonely Street*, New York: Routledge, 1991, 36.

153 Herschel Brickell, 'This is strong men's meat....' (Review of James M. Cain's *The Postman Always Rings Twice*), Syndicated column, February 19, 1934, cited in Roy Hoopes, *Cain*, New York: Holt, Rinehart and Winston, 1982, 596; see also Leff and Simmons, 130–135; Biesen, *Blackout*, 117–119; Biesen, 'Raising Cain with the Censors, Again: *The Postman Always Rings Twice*', *Literature/Film Quarterly*, 28: 1, 2000, 41–48.

154 Leff and Simmons, 130–135.

155 'Love at Laguna Beach', *Life*, 20 August 1945. MGM Studio Press Book Publicity for *The Postman Always Rings Twice* in the USC Press Book Collection and Tay Garnett's Shooting Script for *The Postman Always Rings Twice* in the Tay Garnett Collection, USC Cinematic Arts Library, University of Southern California, Los Angeles, California, 27 April-May 1945–1946, 4.

156 Reverend H. Parr Armstrong, Oklahoma City Council of Churches Letter to Dr. Roswell Barnes in the *MPAA/PCA File*, Academy of Motion Picture Arts and Sciences Library, Beverly Hills, California, 24 August 1945.

157 Joseph I. Breen, 'We believe the finished picture will not be offensive to anyone', Production Code Administration letter to Dr. Samuel McCrea Cavert of the Federal Council of Churches of Christ in America in the *MPAA/PCA File*, Academy of Motion Picture Arts and Sciences Library, Beverly Hills, California, 19 September 1945.

158 Leff and Simmons, 134–135.

159 Ibid.

160 'US Renews Battle on Film Monopolies', *New York Times*, 8 August 1944. For further reading on the Consent Decree, see Jewell; Thomas Brady, 'Hollywood Clears Decks For Consent Decree: Four Studios Revise Production Set-Ups To Meet the New Selling Terms', *New York Times*, 2 March 1941; Douglas W. Churchill, 'Hollywood Changes: Quietly the Major Studios Reorganize Executive Staffs to Meet a New Era', *New York Times*, 6 July 1941.

161 Howard Hawks in Joseph McBride, ed., *Hawks on Hawks*, Lexington: The University of Kentucky Press, 2013, 130–131.

162 Hawks in McBride, *Hawks on Hawks*, 118–119.

163 For further reading, see Mark Harris, *Five Came Back: A Story of Hollywood and the Second World War*, New York: Penguin, 2014.

164 Geoffrey Shurlock, 'The Motion Picture Production Code', *Annals of the American Academy of Political and Social Science*, v. 254, The Motion Picture Industry, November 1947, 140–146.

165 Orson Welles in Fred Stanley, 'An Old Hollywood Costume', *New York Times*, 21 October 1945, X1, 3.

166 'Service Data on Features', *Motion Picture Herald*, 26 July 1947, 3747.

167 The Legion of Decency published books on its Catholic organisation and its ratings of films. National Legion of Decency, *Motion pictures classified by National Legion of Decency: a moral estimate of entertainment feature motion pictures / prepared under the direction of the National Office of the Legion of Decency with the co-operation of the Motion Picture Department of the International Federation of Catholic Alumnae and a male board of consultors*, New York: National Legion of Decency, (5 editions published) 1948–1959.

168 Darryl Zanuck correspondence, Twentieth Century-Fox Collection, University of Southern California, Los Angeles, California, 2 April 1946; see also Rudy Behlmer, *Memo from Darryl F. Zanuck*, New York: Grove Press, 1993, 107–108.

169 MPAA letter to Howard Hughes in the *MPAA/PCA File*, Academy of Motion Picture Arts and Sciences Library, Beverly Hills, California, 9 April 1946.

170 *MPAA/PCA File*, Academy of Motion Picture Arts and Sciences Library, Beverly Hills, California; AFI; USC; *Hollywood Reporter*, 1946–1947; John Cantwell, *The Tidings*, 1947.

171 *MPAA/PCA File*, Academy of Motion Picture Arts and Sciences Library, Beverly Hills, California; AFI; USC; *Hollywood Reporter*, 1946–1947.

172 Ibid.

173 Ibid.

174 *MPAA/PCA File*, Academy of Motion Picture Arts and Sciences Library, Beverly Hills, California; AFI; USC; 1946–1947; *Hollywood Reporter*, February 1947, 1969.

175 Murray Schumach, *The Face on the Cutting Room Floor*, New York: Da Capo, 1975, 139. For further reading regarding this changing post-war climate, see Brian Neve, *Film and Politics in America*, New York: Routledge, 1992. Thomas Doherty observes the blacklisting of Hollywood's creative talent arising from the infamous Waldorf agreement by studios and the motion picture association in 'Reflections on Hollywood's Infamous Blacklist 70 Years Later', *Hollywood Reporter*, 24 November 2017.

176 Schumach, 139; Neve.

177 Joseph I. Breen, Production Code Administration letter to RKO executive William Gordon

in the *MPAA/PCA File*, Academy of Motion Picture Arts and Sciences Library, Beverly Hills, California, 17 July 1945.

178 Joseph I. Breen, Production Code Administration letters to RKO executive William Gordon in the *MPAA/PCA File*, Academy of Motion Picture Arts and Sciences Library, Beverly Hills, California, February 1947.

179 'Crossfire', *New York Times*, AFI, March 1947.

180 AFI; *Ebony*, December 1947.

181 Dore Schary in Robert Porfirio, Alain Silver and James Ursini, *Film Noir Reader 3*, New York: Limelight, 2002, 182.

182 Schary in Porfirio, Silver and Ursini, *Film Noir Reader 3*, 184.

183 Senator Joseph McCarthy insisted he had a list of hundreds of names of Communist sympathisers by 1950. McCarthy's speeches in 1950 deepened the national agenda of anti-Communism and cultural xenophobia, and encouraged the renewal of the HUAC hearings in 1951, while the American Legion was even more significant in this regard. McCarthy also knew John Wayne, President of the Motion Picture Aliance for the Preservation of American Ideals (MPAPAI) from 1949, 'Studios Start Purging Staffs,' *Hollywood Reporter*, 28 November 1947, 1.

184 Stanley Donen in 'Coming Apart', *The Century*, ABC, 2000; see also Tino Balio, ed. *Hollywood in the Age of Television*, Boston: Unwin Hyman, 1990.

185 Darryl Zanuck correspondence, Twentieth Century-Fox Collection, University of Southern California, Los Angeles, California, June-December 1950; see also Behlmer, *Memo from Darryl F. Zanuck*, 174–194.

186 Zanuck, Fox, USC, June-December 1950; Behlmer, *Memo from Darryl F. Zanuck*, 174–194.

187 Ibid.

188 Ibid.

189 Andre de Toth in Robert Porfirio, Alain Silver and James Ursini, *Film Noir Reader 3*, New York: Limelight, 2002, 20.

190 Joseph I. Breen, *MPAA/PCA File*, Academy of Motion Picture Arts and Sciences Library, Beverly Hills, California; Twentieth Century-Fox Collection, University of Southern California, Los Angeles, California, October 1944-December 1947.

191 Otto Preminger in Peter Bogdanovich, ed., *Who the Devil Made It*, New York: Ballantine, 1997, 624.

192 Annette Peyser, NAACP internal memo, NAACP Papers, Library of Congress; AFI; 27 December 1945.

193 Joseph I. Breen, *MPAA/PCA File*, Academy of Motion Picture Arts and Sciences Library, Beverly Hills, California; AFI; 1949.

194 NAACP Papers, Library of Congress; AFI; Zanuck, Fox, USC; Academy of Motion Picture Arts and Sciences Library, Beverly Hills, California, 1948–1949.

195 Lena Horne in *People*, 30 November 1981; George Sidney, letter to the editor, *Los Angeles Times*, 19 December 1981; Lena Horne in *That's Entertainment III*, documentary, 1994.

196 Aljean Harmetz, 'Lena Horne, Sultry Singer,' *New York Times*, 9 May 2010, A1. Lena Horne in *People*, 30 November 1981; Horne, *That's Entertainment III*, 1994; for further reading, see also Sheri Chinen Biesen, *Music in the Shadows: Noir Musical Films*, Baltimore: Johns Hopkins University Press, 2014.

197   Harmetz, 2010, A1; Biesen, *Music in the Shadows*, 2014.

198   Harmetz, 2010, A1; Biesen, *Music in the Shadows*, 2014.

199   NAACP Papers, Library of Congress; AFI; Fox, USC; Academy of Motion Picture Arts and Sciences Library, Beverly Hills, California, 1949–1952.

200   Joseph I. Breen, Father Félix Morlion, *MPAA/PCA File*, Academy of Motion Picture Arts and Sciences Library, Beverly Hills, California; AFI; University of Southern California, Los Angeles, California, 1950. See also Couvares, *Movie Censorship and American Culture*.

201   The 1915 Mutual vs. Ohio decision had, of course, up to that time defined film as a business 'pure and simple', rather than an art form or a communications medium (such as the press) and had laid the groundwork for screen censorship.

202   Preminger in Bogdanovich, *Who the Devil Made It*, 626.

203   Darryl Zanuck, Twentieth Century-Fox Collection, University of Southern California, Los Angeles, California, 23 February 1954; see also, Behlmer, *Memo from Darryl F. Zanuck*, 247–248.

204   Doherty, *Hollywood's Censor*, 6.

205   'Breen Almost Became Generic Name For Code: What Now With Shurlock', *Variety*, 20 October 1954, 20; see also Doherty, *Hollywood's Censor*.

206   Joseph H. Lewis in Robert Porfirio, Alain Silver and James Ursini, eds., *Film Noir Reader 3*, New York: Limelight, 2002, 75. (*Big Combo* star/producer Cornel Wilde was Wallace's real-life husband.)

207   'New Kazan Movie Put On Blacklist; Catholic Legion of Decency Condemns *Baby Doll*—Film Gets Code Seal,' *New York Times*, 28 November 1956.

208   Court decisions confirmed that free speech did not pertain to obscenity. The question was rather one how to define obscenity.

209   Geoffrey Shurlock, MPAA/PCA File, Hitchcock Collection, Academy of Motion Picture Arts and Sciences Library, Beverly Hills, California, November 1959; 19 February-3 March 1960.

210   *Variety*, 4 October 1961, 7; *Variety*, 1 November 1961, 3; AFI; *Daily Variety*, 28 August 1961, 3; *Daily Variety*, 5 October 1961, 4.

211   Vincent Canby, 'Jack Valenti refuses "to become silent movie czar"', *The Globe and Mail*, 10 June 1966, 10.

212   Mark Harris, *Pictures at a Revolution: Five Films and the Birth of New Hollywood*, New York: Penguin, 2008, 182.

213   Harris, *Pictures at a Revolution*, 182–183.

214   Vincent Canby, 'I Don't Remember Seeing Any Really Bad Movies', *New York Times*, 23 April 1967, 42.

215   Geoffrey Shurlock, MPAA/PCA File, Academy of Motion Picture Arts and Sciences Library, Beverly Hills, California, 1967; Shurlock in Harris 194–195; Patrick Goldstein, 'Blasts From the Past', *Los Angeles Times*, 24 August 1997; Biesen, 'Arthur Penn's Bonnie and Clyde as Counterculture Gangster Film: Reimagining Classic Gangster Pictures and Film Noir', in Rebecca Martin, ed., *Critical Insights Film: Bonnie and Clyde*, Ipswich, MA: Salem Press, 2016, 115–133.

216   Harris, 361–362; Biesen, 'Cinematic Comedy and the Swimming Pool: Gender, Class, Coming of Age and Sexual Identity from *The Philadelphia Story* (1940) to *Legally Blonde* (2001)', in Christopher Brown and Pam Hirsch, eds., *The Cinema of the Swimming Pool*,

Berne, Switzerland: Peter Lang, 2014.

217 Hoffman in Harris, 361–362.

218 Harris, 381.

219 Stephen Farber and Estelle Changas, 'Putting the Hex on "R" and "X"', *New York Times*, 9 April 1972.

220 Ibid. Censored films included: *Alice's Restaurant, Little Big Man, THX-1138, Gimme Shelter, A New Leaf, Marriage of a Young Stockbroker, The Last Movie, The Hospital, The Gang That Couldn't Shoot Straight, Diamonds Are Forever, Straw Dogs, Dirty Harry, Macbeth, Sometimes a Great Notion,* and *Dealing: or the Berkeley-to-Boston Forty Brick Lost-Bag Blues.* 'This last-minute editing sometimes involves only a few seconds of film, sometimes a good deal more. Even at its most niggling, the clumsy re-editing affects the rhythm, continuity and impact of individual scenes. At its worst, the board's censorship can alter the meaning of a film. For example, Sam Peckinpah's *Straw Dogs* was originally rated X (No one under 17 admitted) because of the rape scene. It was quite heavily edited for an R (Under 17 requires accompanying parent or adult guardian) ... the board's concerns go beyond details of sex, nudity and language. Rating decisions often implicitly reflect and perpetuate reactionary social attitudes. The predominantly male board had no objections to total female nudity in R films. The male genitalia, more sacred, remained X material—out of bounds even for teen-agers. Rape was sometimes approved in GP films (the unrestricted category recently re-designated PG); normal, pleasurable sex—never. Since no blacks or representatives of other ethnic minority groups have ever served on the board, it is not surprising that rating is based on narrow white middle-class, middle-aged biases.' [CARA subsequently added women of colour to the board.] 'Since they enjoy permanent appointments, their power is virtually unchecked...When Vincent Canby learned that *Alice's Restaurant* was to be re-edited for a GP rating, he perceptively attacked the board's 'carving up of films—an activity that often makes censors feel they are equal partners with the artist in a creative endeavor.' Ironically, we found it was the newer members of the board, particularly the two psychological consultants, who seemed to relish their "creative" contributions. Sitting in the screening room with pen and paper, board members diligently enumerated specific shots, words and scenes that they wanted cut and then often rescreened the "trouble spots" out of context.'

221 *The Exorcist* would later be effectively banned on video in the UK between 1988–1999, when it was denied a video certificate by the BBFC. Roy Meacham, 'Movies', *New York Times*, 3 February 1974, 15.

222 'While I have no doubt that *Jaws* will make a bloody fortune for Universal... it is a coarse-grained and exploitive work which depends on excess for its impact.' Charles Champlin, 'Don't Go Near the Water', *Los Angeles Times*, June 20, 1975.

223 In the 1966 *Memoirs v. Massachusetts* decision, the Supreme Court defined obscenity as 'utterly without redeeming social value', creating a more ambiguous legal climate making it more difficult to define obscenity, and thus allowing greater latitude in content. In the 1973 *Miller v. California* decision, the Supreme Court defined obscenity as 'lacking serious literary, artistic, political or scientific value', based in part on community standards.

224 'Of the 30 top grossing films last year, two were rated G, 17 PG and 11 R.' Moira Hodgson, 'Movie Ratings—Do They Serve Hollywood or The Public', *New York Times*, 24 May 1981, 13.

225 Terri Nash's 1982 Canadian documentary *If You Love This Planet* on medical and social effects of nuclear war became notorious for its clips of Ronald Reagan films, which the US Justice Department labeled 'political propaganda', yet won an Oscar for Best Short Documentary. (Nash thanked the US Government for so effectively 'advertising' her film.) The Pink Pyramid gay and lesbian bookstore in Cincinnati faced fines and prison sentences for obscenity in 1994 over *Salo, or 120 Days of Sodom* (1975) after undercover police rented a videotape of the film. (The prosecutor eventually settled dropping six charges and the store agreed to plead no contest and pay a $500 fine.) Oklahoma City police confiscated *The Tin Drum* (1979) from video stores, the public library and private homes in June 1997 in response to complaints from Oklahomans for Children and Families (OCAF); a federal judge held the film does not contain child pornography and is constitutionally protected because of its artistic value.

226 Signs read: 'Don't Crucify Christ Again', 'Stop This Attack on Christianity' and 'Scripture Not Scripts'.

227 Much like the PCA enforcement of Code censorship vis-à-vis preventing films from being exhibited and released in major theatres.

228 Religious groups pressured video retailers not to stock NC-17 titles, and indeed Blockbuster, Wal-Mart and K-Mart refused to stock the Director's Cut of *Natural Born Killers*.

229 Kenneth Turan, 'Showgirls', *Los Angeles Times*, 22 September 1995.

230 Peter Elkind, 'Sony Pictures: Inside the Hack of the Century, Part 3,' *Fortune*, 1 July 2015.

231 Farber and Changas, 'Putting the Hex on "R" and "X"', *New York Times*, 9 April 1972. Disney and Comcast were battling to acquire Fox in 2017-2018.

232 In terms of demographics, the cinema market—and censorial climate—has transformed since the early 1920s Hays era. Unlike 1924, when MPPDA censors claimed 'movies are an adult entertainment, only 12.5% of audience is under 16' (see MPPDA Digital Archive, mppda.flinders.edu.au/records/182), the MPAA ratings system has encouraged contemporary films, especially blockbusters, to target the youth market audience, even more so than comparatively adult oriented art cinema or independent films.

233 Transnational corporations also acquired independent production companies absorbed into subsidiary arms of massive multinational conglomerates. Chuck Tryon, *On-Demand Culture: Digital Delivery and the Future of Movies*, New Brunswick, N.J.: Rutgers University Press, 2013, 3–4. Sheri Chinen Biesen, 'Binge Watching 'Noir' at Home: Reimagining Cinematic Reception and Distribution via Netflix', in *The Netflix Effect: Technology and Entertainment in the 21st Century*, eds. Kevin McDonald and Daniel Smith-Rowsey, New York: Bloomsbury Academic Publishing, 2016. Schatz observes, 'Conglomeration has intensified the studios' blockbuster mentality while fostering the strategic expansion of established movie 'brands' into worldwide entertainment franchises.' Thomas Schatz, 'Film Industry Studies and Hollywood History' in Jennifer Holt and Alisa Perren, ed. *Media Industries*, Malden, MA: Wiley-Blackwell, 2009, 45.

234 Farah Nayeri, 'Spike Lee and Godard Films to Compete at a Cannes With No Netflix; Cannes Names Contenders As Netflix Boycotts Festival,' *New York Times*, 12 April 2018, C2.

235 Nick Statt, 'Netflix banned from competing at Cannes Film Festival: Netflix Originals can no longer compete for the Palme d'Or,' *The Verge*, 25 March 2018.

236 Eric Kohn, 'Jean-Luc Godard's Sales Agent Says Netflix Should Have Released His New

Film,' *Indiewire*, 3 May 2018.

237 Nayeri, 'Cannes Netflix Boycotts,' *New York Times*, 12 April 2018, C2.

238 Ramin Setoodeh and Brent Lang, 'With Netflix Out and Stars Absent, Will Cannes Remain Influential?', *Variety*, 3 May 2018.

239 Steven Spielberg in David Sims, 'Steven Spielberg's Netflix Fears,' *The Atlantic*, 27 March 2018.

240 Alex Ward, 'Black Panther will be the first film shown in a Saudi movie theater in decades,' *Vox*, 18 April 2018.

241 The Code further specified: 'Vulgarity may be carefully distinguished from obscenity. Vulgarity is the treatment of low, disgusting, unpleasant subjects which decent society considers outlawed from normal conversation. Vulgarity in the motion pictures is limited in precisely the same way as in decent groups of men and women by the dictates of good taste and civilized usage and by the effect of shock, scandal and harm on those coming in contact with this vulgarity. 1. Oaths should never be used as a comedy element. Where required by the plot, the less offensive oaths may be permitted. 2. Vulgar expressions come under the same treatment as vulgarity in general. Where women and children are to see the film, vulgar expressions (and oaths) should be cut to the absolute essentials required by the situation. 3. The name of Jesus Christ should never be used except in reverence.'

242 The Code further specified: 'Obscenity is concerned with immorality, but has the additional connotation of being common, vulgar and coarse. 1. Obscenity in fact, that is, in spoken word, gesture, episode, plot, is against divine and human law and hence altogether outside the range of subject matter or treatment. 2. Obscenity should not be suggested by gesture, manner, etc. 3. An obscene reference, even if it is expected to be understandable to only the more sophisticated part of the audience, should not be introduced. 4. Obscene language is treated as all obscenity.'

243 The Code further specified: 'Ceremonies of any definite religion should be supervised by someone thoroughly conversant with that religion.'

APPENDIX

Reasons Supporting the Preamble of the Code

I. Theatrical motion pictures, that is, pictures intended for the theatre as distinct from pictures intended for churches, schools, lecture halls, educational movements, social reform movements, etc., are primarily to be regarded as ENTERTAINMENT.

Mankind has always recognized the importance of entertainment and its value in rebuilding the bodies and souls of human beings.

But it has always recognized that entertainment can be a character either HELPFUL or HARMFUL to the human race and in consequence has clearly distinguished between:

a. Entertainment which tends to improve the race, or at least to re-create and rebuild human beings exhausted with the realities of life; and

b. Entertainment which tends to degrade human beings, or to lower their standards of life and living.

Hence the MORAL IMPORTANCE of entertainment is something which has been universally recognized. It enters intimately into the lives of men and women and affects them closely; it occupies their minds and affections during leisure hours; and ultimately touches the whole of their lives. A man may be judged by his standard of entertainment as easily as by the standard of his work.

So correct entertainment raises the whole standard of a nation.

Wrong entertainment lowers the whole living conditions and moral ideals of a race.

Note, for example, the healthy reactions to healthful sports, like baseball, golf; the unhealthy reactions to sports like cockfighting, bullfighting, bear baiting, etc.

Note, too, the effect on ancient nations of gladiatorial combats, the obscene plays of Roman times, etc.

II. Motion pictures are very important as ART.

Though a new art, possibly a combination art, it has the same object as the other arts, the presentation of human thought, emotion and experience, in terms of an appeal to the soul through the senses.

Here, as in entertainment,

Art enters intimately into the lives of human beings.

Art can be morally good, lifting men to higher levels. This has been done through good music, great painting, authentic fiction, poetry, drama.

Art can be morally evil it its effects. This is the case clearly enough with unclean art, indecent books, suggestive drama. The effect on the lives of men and women are obvious.

Note: It has often been argued that art itself is unmoral, neither good nor bad. This is true of the THING which is music, painting, poetry, etc. But the THING is the PRODUCT of some person's mind and the intention of that mind was either good or bad morally when it produced the thing. Besides, the thing has its EFFECT upon those who come into contact with it. In both these ways, that is, as a product of a mind and as the cause of definite effects, it has a deep moral significance and unmistakable moral quality.

Hence: The motion pictures, which are the most popular of modern arts for the masses, have their moral quality from the intention of the minds which produce them and from their effects on the moral lives and reactions of their audiences. This gives them a most important morality.

1. They reproduce the morality of the men who use the pictures as a medium for the expression of their ideas and ideals.

2. They affect the moral standards of those who, through the screen, take in these ideas and ideals.

In the case of motion pictures, the effect may be particularly emphasized because no art has so quick and so widespread an appeal to the masses. It has become in an incredibly short period the art of the multitudes.

III. The motion picture, because of its importance as entertainment and because of the trust placed in it by the peoples of the world, has special MORAL OBLIGATIONS:

A. Most arts appeal to the mature. This art appeals at once to every class, mature, immature, developed, undeveloped, law abiding, criminal. Music has its grades for different classes; so has literature and drama. This art of the motion picture, combining as it does the two fundamental appeals of looking at a picture and listening to a story, at once reaches every class of society.

B. By reason of the mobility of film and the ease of picture distribution and because the possibility of duplicating positives in large quantities, this art reaches places unpenetrated by other forms of art.

C. Because of these two facts, it is difficult to produce films intended for only certain classes of people. The exhibitors' theatres are built for the masses, for the cultivated and the rude, the mature and the immature, the self-respecting and the criminal. Films, unlike books and music, can with difficulty be confined to certain selected groups.

D. The latitude given to film material cannot, in consequence, be as wide as the latitude given to book material. In addition:

a. A book describes; a film vividly presents. One presents on a cold page; the other by apparently living people.

b. A book reaches the mind through words merely; a film reaches the eyes and ears through the reproduction of actual events.

c. The reaction of a reader to a book depends largely on the keenness of the reader's imagination; the reaction to a film depends on the vividness of presentation.

Hence many things which might be described or suggested in a book could not possibly be presented in a film.

E. This is also true when comparing the film with the newspaper.

a. Newspapers present by description, films by actual presentation.

b. Newspapers are after the fact and present things as having taken place; the film gives the events in the process of enactment and with apparent reality of life.

F. Everything possible in a play is not possible in a film:

a. Because of the larger audience of the film and its consequential mixed character. Psychologically, the larger the audience, the lower the moral mass resistance to suggestion.

b. Because through light, enlargement of character, presentation, scenic emphasis, etc., the screen story is brought closer to the audience than the play.

c. The enthusiasm for and interest in the film actors and actresses, developed beyond anything of the sort in history, makes the audience largely sympathetic toward the characters they portray and the stories in which they figure. Hence the audience is more ready to confuse actor and actress and the characters they portray and it is most receptive of the emotions and ideals presented by the favorite stars.

G. Small communities, remote from sophistication and from the hardening process which often takes place in the ethical and moral standards of larger cities, are easily and readily reached by any sort of film.

H. The grandeur of mass settings, large action, spectacular features, etc., affects and arouses more intensely the emotional side of the audience.

In general, the mobility, popularity, accessibility, emotional appeal, vividness, straightforward presentation of fact in the film make for more intimate contact with a larger audience and for greater emotional appeal.

Hence the larger moral responsibilities of the motion pictures.

Reasons Underlying the General Principles

I. No picture shall be produced which will lower the moral standards of those who see it. Hence the sympathy of the audience should never be thrown to the side of crime, wrongdoing, evil or sin.

This is done:

1. When evil is made to appear attractive and alluring and good is made to appear unattractive.

2. When the sympathy of the audience is thrown on the side of crime, wrongdoing, evil, sin. The same is true of a film that would thrown sympathy against goodness, honor, innocence, purity or honesty.

Note: Sympathy with a person who sins is not the same as sympathy with the sin or crime of which he is guilty. We may feel sorry for the plight of the murderer or even understand the circumstances which led him to his crime: we may not feel sympathy with the wrong which he has done. The presentation of evil is often essential for art or fiction or drama. This in itself is not wrong provided:

a. That evil is not presented alluringly. Even if later in the film the evil is condemned or punished, it must not be allowed to appear so attractive that the audience's emotions are drawn to desire or approve so strongly that later the condemnation is forgotten and only the apparent joy of sin is remembered.

b. That throughout, the audience feels sure that evil is wrong and good is right.

II. Correct standards of life shall, as far as possible, be presented.

A wide knowledge of life and of living is made possible through the film. When right standards are consistently presented, the motion picture exercises the most powerful influences. It builds character, develops right ideals, inculcates correct principles and all this in attractive story form.

If motion pictures consistently hold up for admiration high types of characters and present stories that will affect lives for the better, they can become the most powerful force for the improvement of mankind.

III. Law, natural or human, shall not be ridiculed, nor shall sympathy be created for its violation.

By natural law is understood the law which is written in the hearts of all mankind, the greater underlying principles of right and justice dictated by conscience.

By human law is understood the law written by civilized nations.

1. The presentation of crimes against the law is often necessary for the carrying out of the plot. But the presentation must not throw sympathy with the crime as against the law nor with the criminal as against those who punish him.

2. The courts of the land should not be presented as unjust. This does not mean that a single court may not be presented as unjust, much less that a single court official must not be presented this way. But the court system of the country must not suffer as a result of this presentation.

Reasons Underlying the Particular Applications

I. Sin and evil enter into the story of human beings and hence in themselves are valid dramatic material.

II. In the use of this material, it must be distinguished between sin which repels by its very nature and sins which often attract.

a. In the first class come murder, most theft, many legal crimes, lying, hypocrisy, cruelty, etc.

b. In the second class come sex sins, sins and crimes of apparent heroism, such as banditry, daring thefts, leadership in evil, organized crime, revenge, etc.

The first class needs less care in treatment, as sins and crimes of this class are naturally unattractive. The audience instinctively condemns all such and is repelled.

Hence the important objective must be to avoid the hardening of the audience, especially of those who are young and impressionable, to the thought and fact of crime. People can become accustomed even to murder, cruelty, brutality and repellent crimes, if these are too frequently repeated.

The second class needs great care in handling, as the response of human nature to their appeal is obvious. This is treated more fully below.

III. A careful distinction can be made between films intended for general distribution and films intended for use in theatres restricted to a limited audience. Themes and plots quite appropriate for the latter would be altogether out of place and dangerous in the former.

Note: The practice of using a general theatre and limiting its patronage to 'Adults Only' is not completely satisfactory and is only partially effective.

However, maturer minds may easily understand and accept without harm subject matter in plots which do younger people positive harm.

Hence: If there should be created a special type of theatre, catering exclusively to an adult audience, for plays of this character (plays with problem themes, difficult discussions and maturer treatment) it would seem to afford an outlet, which does not now exist, for pictures unsuitable for general distribution but permissible for exhibitions to a restricted audience.

I. Crimes Against the Law

The treatment of crimes against the law must not:

1. Teach methods of crime.
2. Inspire potential criminals with a desire for imitation.
3. Make criminals seem heroic and justified.

Revenge in modern times shall not be justified. In lands and ages of less developed civilization and moral principles, revenge may sometimes be presented. This would be the case especially in places where no law exists to cover the crime because of which revenge is committed.

Because of its evil consequences, the drug traffic should not be presented in any form. The existence of the trade should not be brought to the attention of audiences.

The use of liquor should never be excessively presented. In scenes from American life, the necessities of plot and proper characterization alone justify its use. And in this case, it should be shown with moderation.

II. Sex

Out of a regard for the sanctity of marriage and the home, the triangle, that is, the love of a third party for one already married, needs careful handling. The treatment should not throw sympathy against marriage as an institution.

Scenes of passion must be treated with an honest acknowledgement of human nature and its normal reactions. Many scenes cannot be presented without arousing dangerous emotions on the part of the immature, the young or the criminal classes.

Even within the limits of pure love, certain facts have been universally regarded by lawmakers as outside the limits of safe presentation.

In the case of impure love, the love which society has always regarded as wrong and which has been banned by divine law, the following are important:

1. Impure love must not be presented as attractive and beautiful.
2. It must not be the subject of comedy or farce, or treated as material for laughter.
3. It must not be presented in such a way to arouse passion or morbid curiosity on the part of the audience.
4. It must not be made to seem right and permissible.
5. It general, it must not be detailed in method and manner.

III. Vulgarity;[241] IV. Obscenity;[242] V. Profanity; hardly needs further explanation than is contained in the Code.

VI. Costume

General Principles:

1. The effect of nudity or semi-nudity upon the normal man or woman and much more upon the young and upon immature persons, has been honestly recognized by all lawmakers and moralists.
2. Hence the fact that the nude or semi-nude body may be beautiful does not make its use in the films moral. For, in addition to its beauty, the effect of the nude or semi-nude body on the normal individual must be taken into consideration.
3. Nudity or semi-nudity used simply to put a 'punch' into a picture comes under the head of immoral actions. It is immoral in its effect on the average audience.
4. Nudity can never be permitted as being necessary for the plot. Semi-nudity must not result in undue or indecent exposures.
5. Transparent or translucent materials and silhouette are frequently more suggestive

than actual exposure.

PARTICULAR PRINCIPLES:

(1) The more intimate parts of the human body are male and female organs and the breasts of a woman.

(a) They should never be uncovered.

(b) They should not be covered with transparent or translucent material.

(c) They should not be clearly and unmistakably outlined by the garment.

(2) The less intimate parts of the body the legs, arms, shoulders and back, are less certain of causing reactions on the part of the audience.

Hence:

(a) Exposure necessary for the plot or action is permitted.

(b) Exposure for the sake of exposure or the 'punch' is wrong.

(c) Scenes of undressing should be avoided. When necessary for the plot, they should be kept within the limits of decency. When not necessary for the plot, they are to be avoided, as their effect on the ordinary spectator is harmful.

(d) The manner or treatment of exposure should not be suggestive or indecent.

(e) The following is important in connection with dancing costumes:

1. Dancing costumes cut to permit grace or freedom of movement, provided they remain within the limits of decency indicated are permissible.

2. Dancing costumes cut to permit indecent actions or movements or to make possible during the dance indecent exposure, are wrong, especially when permitting:

a) Movements of the breasts;

b) Movements or sexual suggestions of the intimate parts of the body;

c) Suggestion of nudity.

VII. Dances

(1) Dancing in general is recognized as an art and a beautiful form of expressing human emotion.

(2) Obscene dances are those:

(a) Which suggest or represent sexual actions, whether performed solo or with two or more;

(b) Which are designed to excite an audience, to arouse passions, or to cause physical excitement.

HENCE: Dances of the type known as 'Kooch', or 'Can-Can', since they violate decency in these two ways, are wrong. Dances with movements of the breasts, excessive body movement while the feet remain stationary, the so-called 'belly dances'—these dances are immoral, obscene and hence altogether wrong.

VIII. Religion

The reason why ministers of religion may not be comic characters or villains is simply because the attitude taken toward them may easily become the attitude taken toward religion in general. Religion is lowered in the minds of the audience because of the lowering of the audience's respect for a minister.[243]

IX. Locations

Certain places are so closely and thoroughly associated with sexual life or with sexual sin that their use must be carefully limited.

(1) Brothels and houses of ill-fame no matter of what country, are not proper locations for drama. They suggest to the average person at once sex sin, or they excite an unwhole-

some and morbid curiosity in the minds of youth.

IN GENERAL: They are dangerous and bad dramatic locations.

(2) Bedrooms. In themselves they are perfectly innocent. Their suggestion may be kept innocent. However, under certain situations they are bad dramatic locations.

(a) Their use in a comedy or farce (on the principle of the so called bedroom farce) is wrong, because they suggest sex laxity and obscenity.

(b) In serious drama, their use should, where sex is suggested, be confined to absolute essentials, in accordance with the principles laid down above.

X. National Feelings

The just rights, history and feelings of any nation are entitled to most careful consideration and respectful treatment.

XI. Titles

As the title of a picture is the brand on that particular type of goods, it must conform to the ethical practices of all such honest business.

XII. Repellent Subjects

Such subjects are occasionally necessary for the plot. Their treatment must never offend good taste nor injure the sensibilities of an audience.

BIBLIOGRAPHY

A Code to Govern the Making of Talking, Synchronized and Silent Motion Pictures. Formulated by The Association of Motion Picture Producers, Inc. and The Motion Picture Producers and Distributors of America, Inc., March 1930.

Abel, Richard, ed., *Silent Film*. New Brunswick, NJ: Rutgers University Press, 1995.

____, *Encyclopedia of Early Cinema*. London: Taylor & Francis, 2005.

'Advertising Code of Ethics.' In *Film Daily Year Book*. New York: The Film Daily, 1931, 663.

Allan, Bruce. 'British Take Critical View of Code Talks: Some Editors Satirical On U. S. Film Morals,' *Motion Picture Daily*, 16 May 1935, 1, 4.

Arnheim, Rudolph. In Marilyn Yaquinto, *Pump 'Em Full of Lead: A Look at Gangsters on Film*. New York: Twayne, 1998.

Balcon, Michael. In *Motion Picture Daily*, 20 April 1935.

Balio, Tino, ed. *Hollywood in the Age of Television*. Boston: Unwin Hyman, 1990.

____. *Grand Design*. New York: Scribners, 1993.

Barnes, Brooks and John Koblin. 'Disney's Big Bet on Streaming Relies on Little-Known Tech Company,' *New York Times*, October 8, 2017.

Barnes, Brooks and Michael Cieply. 'Sony Drops *The Interview* Following Terrorist Threats.' *New York Times*, 18 December 2014, B1.

Behlmer, Rudy. *Memo From David O. Selznick*. New York: Viking Press, 1972.

____, ed. *Inside Warner Bros. (1935–1951)*. New York: Viking Penguin, 1985.

____. *Memo from Darryl F. Zanuck*, New York: Grove Press, 1993.

Bernstein, Matthew. 'A Tale of Three Cities: The Banning of *Scarlet Street*', *Cinema Journal*, 35.1, 1995, 27–52.

____, ed., *Controlling Hollywood: Censorship and Regulation in the Studio Era*. New Brunswick, NJ: Rutgers University Press, 1999.

Biesen, Sheri Chinen. 'Censorship, Film Noir and *Double Indemnity*,' *Film & History* 25: 1–2, 1995, 40–52.

____. 'Raising Cain with the Censors, Again: *The Postman Always Rings Twice*,' *Literature/*

Film Quarterly 28: 1, 2000, 41–48.

____. *Blackout: World War II and the Origins of Film Noir*. Baltimore: Johns Hopkins University Press, 2005.

____. 'Cinematic Comedy and the Swimming Pool: Gender, Class, Coming of Age and Sexual Identity from *The Philadelphia Story* (1940) to *Legally Blonde* (2001).' In Christopher Brown and Pam Hirsch, eds., *The Cinema of the Swimming Pool*. Berne, Switzerland: Peter Lang, 2014.

____. *Music in the Shadows: Noir Musical Films,* Baltimore: Johns Hopkins University Press, 2014.

____. 'Binge Watching "Noir" at Home: Reimagining Cinematic Reception and Distribution via Netflix.' In Kevin McDonald and Daniel Smith-Rowsey, eds. *The Netflix Effect: Technology and Entertainment in the 21st Century*. New York: Bloomsbury Academic Publishing, 2016.

____. 'Arthur Penn's Bonnie and Clyde as Counterculture Gangster Film: Reimagining Classic Gangster Pictures and Film Noir.' In Rebecca Martin, ed., *Critical Insights Film: Bonnie and Clyde*. Ipswich, MA: Salem Press, 2016.

Black, Gregory D. 'Hollywood Censored: The Production Code Administration and the Hollywood Film Industry, 1930–1940,' *Film History* 3.3, 1989, 167–189.

____. *Hollywood Censored: Morality Codes, Catholics and the Movies*. Cambridge: Cambridge University Press, 1994.

Blum, John Morton. *V Was for Victory: Politics and American Culture During World War II*. San Diego: Harcourt Brace Jovanovich, 1976.

Bogdanovich, Peter, ed. *Who the Devil Made It*. New York: Ballantine, 1997.

'Breen Almost Became Generic Name For Code: What Now With Shurlock,' *Variety*, 20 October 1954, 20.

Brady, Thomas. 'Hollywood Clears Decks For Consent Decree: Four Studios Revise Production Set-Ups To Meet the New Selling Terms,' *New York Times*, 2 March 1941.

Brickell, Herschel. 'This is strong men's meat....' (Review of James M. Cain's *The Postman Always Rings Twice*), Syndicated column, February 19, 1934. In Roy Hoopes, *Cain*. New York: Holt, Rinehart and Winston, 1982, 596.

Cain, James M. In David Hanna, 'Hays Censors Rile Jim Cain,' *Daily News* (Los Angeles), 14 February 1944, 11–13.

____. In Lloyd Shearer, 'Crime Certainly Pays on the Screen: The growing crop of homicidal films poses questions for psychologists and producers,' *New York Times*, 8 August 1945.

Canby, Vincent. 'Jack Valenti refuses "to become silent movie czar,"' *The Globe and Mail*, 10 June 1966, 10.

____. 'I Don't Remember Seeing Any Really Bad Movies,' *New York Times*, 23 April 1967, 42.

Cantwell, John. *The Tidings*, 1947.

Carr, Steven Alan. 'Inside the Chicago Exhibition of *Inside Nazi Germany* (RKO, 1938).' Society for Cinema and Media Studies, 2017.

Casper, Drew. *Postwar Hollywood*. Malden, MA: Blackwell, 2007.

'Catholics Approve Two Debated Films,' *New York Times*, 6 July 1936.

Champlin, Charles. 'Don't Go Near the Water,' *Los Angeles Times*, June 20, 1975.

'Chaplin is Called for Movie Inquiry: Senators Will Ask Inquiry on *The Great Dictator*,' *New York Times*, 14 September 1941, 41.

'Church Tightens On Pix,' *Variety*, 11 December 1935, 3.

Churchill, Douglas W. 'Hollywood Changes: Quietly the Major Studios Reorganize Executive Staffs to Meet a New Era,' *New York Times*, 6 July 1941.

Courtney, Susan. *Hollywood Fantasies of Miscegenation: Spectacular Narratives of Gender and Race*. Princeton: Princeton University Press, 2004.

Couvares, Francis. 'The Good Censor: Race, sex, and censorship in the early cinema,' *Yale Journal of Criticism* 7: 2, 1994.

_____, ed., *Movie Censorship and American Culture*. Washington: Smithsonian, 1996; Amherst: University of Massachusetts Press, 2006.

'Crossfire,' *New York Times*, March 1947.

Cukor, George. In Peter Bogdanovich, ed. *Who the Devil Made It*. New York: Ballantine, 1997.

Curry, Ramona. 'Mae West as Censored Commodity: The Case of *Klondike Annie*,' *Cinema Journal* 31.1, 1991, 57–85.

Dietrich, Marlene. Interviewed by William Mooring, *London Film Weekly*, 1935.

Doherty, Thomas. *Projections of War: Hollywood, American Culture and World War II*. New York: Columbia University Press, 1993.

_____. *Pre-Code Hollywood: Sex, Immorality and Insurrection in American Cinema, 1930–1934*. New York: Columbia University Press, 1999.

_____. 'The Code Before "Da Vinci,"' *Washington Post*, May 20, 2006.

_____. *Hollywood's Censor: Joseph I. Breen and the Production Code Administration*. New York: Columbia University Press, 2009.

_____. *Hollywood and Hitler, 1933–1939*. New York: Columbia University Press, 2013.

_____. 'Reflections on Hollywood's Infamous Blacklist 70 Years Later,' *Hollywood Reporter*, 24 November 2017.

Donen, Stanley. In 'Coming Apart,' *The Century*, ABC Documentary, 2000.

Donohue, H. E. F. 'Remembrance of Murders Past: An Interview With Alfred Hitchcock.' *New York Times*, 14 December 1969.

'*Double Indemnity* Drama of Knockout Proportions,' *Hollywood Reporter*, 24 April 1944.

Dwan, Allan. In Peter Bogdanovich, ed. *Who the Devil Made It*. New York: Ballantine, 1997.

Elkind, Peter. 'Sony Pictures: Inside the Hack of the Century, Part 3,' *Fortune*, 1 July 2015.

'Famous Players-Lasky Ban Sex Films By Fourteen "Don'ts" To Studio Officials...Crime and Underworld Stuff Allowable When It Serves a Moral Purpose—Illicit Love Forbidden.' *Variety* LXI: 13, 18 February 1921, 46.

Farber, Stephen and Estelle Changas. 'Putting the Hex on "R" and "X"', *New York Times*, 9 April 1972.

'Fight of Century, Says Jack London,' *Philadelphia Inquirer*, 2 July 1910, 10.

Goldstein, Patrick. 'Blasts From the Past,' *Los Angeles Times*, 24 August 1997.

Grieveson, Lee. *Policing Cinema: Movies and Censorship in Early-Twentieth Century America*. Berkeley: University of California Press, 2004.

Harmetz, Aljean. *Round Up the Usual Suspects: The Making of Casablanca*, New York:

Hyperion, 1992.

____. *On the Road to Tara*. New York: Abrams, 1996.

____. 'Lena Horne, Sultry Singer,' *New York Times*, 9 May 2010, A1.

Harris, Mark. *Pictures at a Revolution: Five Films and the Birth of New Hollywood*. New York: Penguin, 2008.

____. *Five Came Back: A Story of Hollywood and the Second World War*. New York: Penguin, 2014.

Hawks, Howard. In Joseph McBride, ed. *Hawks on Hawks*. Lexington: The University of Kentucky Press, 2013.

Hitchcock, Alfred. 'Master of Suspense: A Self-Analysis.' *New York Times*, 1950.

____. In *Hitchcock S'Explique*, French documentary, André S. Labarthe, 1965.

Hodgson, Moira. 'Movie Ratings—Do They Serve Hollywood or The Public,' *New York Times*, 24 May 1981, 13.

Hoopes, Roy. *Cain*. New York: Holt, Rinehart and Winston, 1982.

Horne, Lena. In *People*, 30 November 1981.

____. In *That's Entertainment III*, documentary, 1994.

Jacobs, Lea. 'The Censorship of the Blonde Venus,' *Cinema Journal*, 27, 1988, 21–31.

____. *The Wages of Sin: Censorship and the Fallen Woman Film, 1928–1942*. Madison: University of Wisconsin Press, 1991.

Jewell, Richard B. *The Golden Age of Cinema*. New York: Blackwell, 2007.

Jewell, Richard B. and Vernon Harbin, *The RKO Story*, London: Arlington Press, 1982.

Johnson, David. *Lavender Scare*. Chicago: University of Chicago Press, 2004.

Kiarostami, Abbas. In Michel Ciment, *Film World: Interviews with cinema's leading directors*. New York: Berg Publishers, 2009.

King, Homay. *Lost in Translation*. Durham, NC: Duke University Press, 2010.

Kitamura, Hiroshi. *Screening Enlightenment: Hollywood and the Cultural Reconstruction of Defeated Japan*. Ithaca: Cornell University Press, 2010.

Kohn, Eric. 'Jean-Luc Godard's Sales Agent Says Netflix Should Have Released His New Film,' *Indiewire*, 3 May 2018.

Koppes, Clayton R. and Gregory D. Black. *Hollywood Goes to War: How Politics, Profits and Propaganda Shaped World War II Movies*. New York: The Free Press, 1987.

Koppes, Clayton. 'Show Stoppers: Movie Censorship Considered as a Business Proposition.' *Essays in Economic and Business History* 30, 2012, 63–76.

Krutnik, Frank. *In a Lonely Street*. New York: Routledge, 1991.

Kuhn, Annette. *Cinema, Censorship and Sexuality*. London: Routledge, 1988.

Kurosawa, Akira. In Audie Bock, 'Kurosawa on His Innovative Cinema.' *New York Times*, 4 October 1981.

____. *Something Like an Autobiography*. New York: Vintage, 1983.

Leff, Leonard and Jerold Simmons. *The Dame In The Kimono: Hollywood, Censorship and the Production Code from the 1920s to the 1960s*. New York: Grove, 1990; reprinted by Lexington: University of Kentucky Press, 2001.

Lev, Peter. *The Fifties*. New York: Scribners, 2003.

Lewis, Jon. *Hollywood v. Hard-Core*. New York: New York University Press, 2000.

Lewis, Joseph H. In Robert Porfirio, Alain Silver and James Ursini, eds., *Film Noir Reader 3*.

New York: Limelight, 2002.

Lord, Daniel A. *Played By Ear: The Autobiography of Daniel A. Lord, S. J.* Chicago: Loyola University Press, 1955.

'Love at Laguna Beach,' *Life*, 20 August 1945.

Maltby, Richard. *Harmless Entertainment: Hollywood and the Ideology of Consensus.* Metuchen, NJ: Scarecrow, 1983.

____. 'To Prevent the Prevalent Type of Book: Censorship and Adaptation in Hollywood, 1924–1934,' *American Quarterly* 44.4, 1992.

McBride, Joseph, ed. *Hawks on Hawks.* Lexington: University of Kentucky Press, 2013.

Meacham, Roy. 'Movies', *New York Times*, 3 February 1974, 15.

Mellett, Lowell. 1942, in *1944 Appropriation Hearings*, 937–940. In Cedric Larson, 'The Domestic Motion Picture Work of the Office of War Information,' *Hollywood Quarterly* 3.4, 1948, 440.

Moley, Raymond. *The Hays Office*, New York: Bobbs-Merrill, 1945.

'The Motion Picture Production Code.' 31 March 1930, reprinted in Terry Ramsaye, 'What the Production Code Really Means,' *Motion Picture Herald*, 11 August 1934, 10–13.

'The Motion Picture Production Code.' 31 March 1930, reprinted in Richard Maltby, *Hollywood Cinema*. Oxford: Blackwell, 2003.

National Legion of Decency, *Motion pictures classified by National Legion of Decency: a moral estimate of entertainment feature motion pictures / prepared under the direction of the National Office of the Legion of Decency with the co-operation of the Motion Picture Department of the International Federation of Catholic Alumnae and a male board of consultors*, New York: National Legion of Decency, (5 editions published), 1948–1959.

Nayeri, Farah. 'Spike Lee and Godard Films to Compete at a Cannes With No Netflix; Cannes Names Contenders As Netflix Boycotts Festival,' *New York Times*, 12 April 2018, C2.

Neve, Brian. *Film and Politics in America.* New York: Routledge, 1992.

'New Films For "Screen" Machines,' *The Phonoscope* 3.1, 1899, 15.

'New Kazan Movie Put On Blacklist; Catholic Legion of Decency Condemns *Baby Doll*— Film Gets Code Seal,' *New York Times*, 28 November 1956.

'Newsreels to Huddle on Nazi Outrages,' *Film Daily*, 17 November 1938.

Noreiga, Chon. '"Something's Missing Here!": Homosexuality and Film Reviews during the Production Code Era, 1934–1962,' *Cinema Journal* 30: 1, 1990, 20–41.

Orbach, Barak Y. 'The Johnson-Jeffries Fight and Censorship of Black Supremacy.' *New York University Journal of Law & Liberty* 5: 270, 2010, 270–346.

Orbach, Barak Y. 'Prizefighting and the Birth of Movie Censorship.' *Yale Journal of Law and the Humanities* 21: 2, Art 3, 2009, 251–304.

Porfirio, Robert, Alain Silver and James Ursini, eds., *Film Noir Reader 3*. New York: Limelight, 2002.

Preminger, Otto. In Peter Bogdanovich, ed. *Who the Devil Made It*. New York: Ballantine, 1997.

'Producers Take Drastic Step to Assure 100 Per Cent. Clean Screen Productions.' *Moving Picture World*, 19 March 1921, 240–241.

Quicke, Andrew. 'The Era of Censorship (1930–1967).' In *The Routledge Companion to Religion and Film*. John Lyden, ed., 2009; reprinted by New York: Taylor and Francis-Routledge, 2010, 32–51.

Robinson, Edward G. In Bosley Crowther, 'Little Caesar Waits His Chance,' *New York Times*, 22 January 1939.

Ragone, August. *Eiji Tsuburaya: Master of Monsters*, San Francisco: Chronicle Books, 2014.

Regester, Charlene. 'Black Screen/White Censors.' In Francis Couvares, ed., *Movie Censorship and American Culture*, Washington: Smithsonian, 1996; reprinted by Amherst: University of Massachusetts Press, 2006.

'Religion: Legion of Decency,' *Time*, 11 June 1934.

Ross, Steven J. '*Confessions of a Nazi Spy*: Warner Bros., Anti-Fascism and the Politicization of Hollywood.' In Martin Kaplan and Johanna Blakley, eds., *Warners' War: Politics, Pop Culture and Propaganda In Wartime Hollywood*. Norman Lear Center Press, University of Southern California, Los Angeles, 2004, 48–59.

Schatz, Thomas. *Hollywood Genres,* New York: McGraw-Hill, 1981.

____. *The Genius of the System*. New York: Pantheon, 1988, 1996.

____. *Boom and Bust: American Cinema in the 1940s*. New York: Scribners, 1997.

____. 'Film Industry Studies and Hollywood History.' In Jennifer Holt and Alisa Perren, eds. *Media Industries*, Malden, MA: Wiley-Blackwell, 2009.

Scheuer, Philip. 'Film History Made by *Double Indemnity*,' *Los Angeles Times,* 6 August 1944, 1, 3.

Schumach, Murray. *The Face on the Cutting Room Floor*. New York: Da Capo, 1975.

Scott, Ellen. *Cinema Civil Rights: Regulation, Repression, and Race in the Classical Hollywood Era*. New Brunswick, NJ: Rutgers University Press, 2015.

Schary, Dore. In Robert Porfirio, Alain Silver and James Ursini, eds., *Film Noir Reader 3*. New York: Limelight, 2002.

Selznick, David O. In Rudy Behlmer, ed. *Memo From David O. Selznick*. New York: Viking Press, 1972.

'Service Data on Features,' *Motion Picture Herald*, 26 July 1947, 3747.

Setoodeh, Ramin and Brent Lang. 'With Netflix Out and Stars Absent, Will Cannes Remain Influential?' *Variety*, 3 May 2018.

Shearer, Lloyd. 'Crime Certainly Pays on the Screen: The growing crop of homicidal films poses questions for psychologists and producers,' *New York Times*, 8 August 1945.

Sherry, Michael. *Gay Artists in Modern American Culture*. Chapel Hill: University of North Carolina Press, 2007.

Shurlock, Geoffrey. 'The Motion Picture Production Code,' *Annals of the American Academy of Political and Social Science*, 254, The Motion Picture Industry, November 1947, 140–146.

Sidney, George. Letter to the editor, *Los Angeles Times*, 19 December 1981.

Spielberg, Steven. In David Sims, 'Steven Spielberg's Netflix Fears,' *The Atlantic*, 27 March 2018.

Stamp, Shelley. 'Moral Coercion, or the Board of Censorship Ponders the Vice Question.' In *Controlling Hollywood: Censorship and Regulation in the Studio Era*, Matthew Bernstein, ed., New Brunswick, NJ: Rutgers University Press, 1999.

Stanley, Fred. 'Hollywood Peeks Into the Future,' *New York Times*, 21 February 1943.
____. 'Hollywood Turns To "Hate" Films: Government Lifts Ban on Showing Jap Brutality—Various Other Matters,' *New York Times*, 6 February 1944.
____. 'News From Hollywood,' *New York Times*, 21 March 1944.
____. 'Hollywood Crime and Romance', *New York Times*, 19 November 1944.
____. 'An Old Hollywood Costume,' *New York Times*, 21 October 1945, X1, 3.
Statt, Nick. 'Netflix banned from competing at Cannes Film Festival: Netflix Originals can no longer compete for the Palme d'Or,' *The Verge*, 25 March 2018.
Streible, Dan. 'Race and Reception of Jack Johnson Fight Films.' In Daniel Bernandi ed., *The Birth of Whiteness: Race and the Emergence of U.S. Cinema*. New Brunswick, NJ: Rutgers University Press, 1996.
____. *Fight Pictures—A History of Boxing and Early Cinema*. Berkeley: University of California Press, 2008.
'Studios Start Purging Staffs,' *Hollywood Reporter*, 28 November 1947, 1.
Trumpbour, John. *Selling Hollywood to the World: US and European Struggles for Mastery of the Global Film Industry, 1920–1950*. New York: Cambridge University Press, 2002.
Turan, Kenneth. 'Showgirls,' *Los Angeles Times*, 22 September 1995.
Tryon, Chuck. *On-Demand Culture: Digital Delivery and the Future of Movies*. New Brunswick, N.J.: Rutgers University Press, 2013.
'US Renews Battle on Film Monopolies,' *New York Times*, 8 August 1944.
Walsh, Frank. *Sin and Censorship: The Catholic Church and the Motion Picture Industry*. New Haven: Yale University Press, 1996.
Ward, Alex. 'Black Panther will be the first film shown in a Saudi movie theater in decades,' *Vox*, 18 April 2018.
Ward, Geoffrey. *Unforgivable Blackness*. New York: Alfred Knopf, 2004. (see also Ken Burns PBS documentary.)
Welles, Orson. In Fred Stanley, 'An Old Hollywood Costume,' *New York Times*, 21 October 1945, X1, 3.
White, Patricia. *Uninvited*. Bloomington: Indiana University Press, 1999.
Winkler, Allan. *The Politics of Propaganda: The Office of War Information, 1942–1945*. New Haven: Yale University Press, 1978.
Zanuck, Darryl F. In Rudy Behlmer, ed. *Memo from Darryl F. Zanuck*. New York: Grove Press, 1993.

INDEX